the NBA finals

MARK STEWART

Researched and Edited by
MIKE KENNEDY

FRANKLIN WATTS
A Division of Scholastic Inc.
New York • Toronto • London • Auckland • Sydney
Mexico City • New Delhi • Hong Kong
Danbury, Connecticut

Cover design by Dave Klaboe   Series design by Molly Heron

Cover photo ID's: (center left) Gary Payton; (center right) the New York Knicks forward, Dave DeBusschere; (clockwise from upper left) Kobe Bryant taking the ball to the hoop; Michael Jordan of the Chicago Bulls; Allen Iverson playing for the Philadelphia 76ers; the formidable Los Angeles Lakers center, Shaquille O'Neal; Charles Barkley's 1992 Topps Stadium trading card; the Detroit Piston's star point guard, Isiah Thomas; Willis Reed and Wilt Chamberlain on the cover of the official 1970-71 *National Basketball Association Guide*; Bob Cousy, point guard for the Boston Celtics.

Photographs © 2003: AP/Wide World Photos: 79 (Rick Bowmer), 86 (Kevork Djansezian), 85 (Ron Frehm), 78, 82 (Beth A. Keiser), cover top right (Rusty Kennedy), 70 (Doug Pizac), 18, 57, 65; Basketball Hall of Fame, Springfield, MA: 4, 7, 9, 10, 11, 17, 19 right, 19 left, 23, 25, 29, 52, 53; Corbis Images: 13 bottom, 13 top, 21, 31, 41, 44, 62, 68, 73 (Bettmann), 90 (Adrees Latif/Reuters NewMedia Inc.), cover top center (William Sallaz/Duomo); Getty Images: cover top left, cover bottom right (Lisa Blumenfeld), 27, 43 (Walter Iooss Jr./NBAE), 22 (NBA Photos/NBAE), 48 (Rich Pilling/NBAE), 63 (Rick Stewart); Team Stewart, Inc.: cover bottom center left, cover bottom left, cover center right, cover center left, cover bottom center right, cover center, 12, 16, 34, 36, 38, 45, 51, 60, 77, 81.

Library of Congress Cataloging-in-Publication Data

Stewart, Mark, 1960-
    The NBA finals / by Mark Stewart; researched and edited by Mike Kennedy.
    p. cm. — (The Watts history of sports)
    Summary: Looks at the history of the National Basketball Association's
    annual best-of-seven game series to determine the championship of the
    league, which has been held since the 1940s.
    Includes bibliographical references (p.) and index.
    ISBN 0-531-11955-6
    1. National Basketball Association—History—Juvenile literature.
    [1. National Basketball Association. 2. Basketball.] I. Kennedy, Mike (Mike William),
    1965- II. Title. III. Series.
    GV885.515.N37S76 2003
    797.323'64—dc21   2003005815

CONTENTS

Joe Fulks of the Warriors, whose pioneering use of the jumpshot gave NBA fans a preview of things to come.

INTRODUCTION

Bright Lights, Big Cities

In the years following World War II, there were high hopes for the future of professional basketball. College hoops had always been popular, but the pro game never got off the ground after a promising start in the 1920s. The Great Depression of the 1930s and then the war had put this great experiment on hold for 15 years. Finally, in the summer of 1946, a group of investors got together and formed the BAA—Basketball Association of America—the forerunner of today's NBA. The team owners all operated sports arenas in major cities: Boston, Chicago, Cleveland, Detroit, New York, Pittsburgh, Philadelphia, Providence, Toronto, and Washington, DC. They hoped to draw the same large crowds that already paid high prices to see college tournaments, ice hockey games, circuses, and other special events.

Unfortunately for the BAA, the nation's best basketball players were already performing in the National Basketball League, which had been limping along since the late 1930s. Most of the NBL franchises were located in smaller cities, between the Mississippi River and the Appalachian Mountains, such as Sheboygan and Fort Wayne. They drew good crowds, and the cities loved their teams. The players were big celebrities and were paid well for their talents. For several years, the BAA was forced to play catch-up. It was able to narrow the talent gap by out-bidding NBL teams for the top college players, but the clubs lost a lot of money playing to small crowds in huge arenas. Many franchises folded in these years, and success was never guaranteed.

The first BAA championship was played in the spring of 1947 between the Philadelphia Warriors and the Chicago Stags. The Warriors, led by Joe Fulks, were crowned league champions after winning four of five games against Chicago. The NBL champions, Chicago Gears, starring the enormous George Mikan, probably would have killed the Warriors had they played. The Baltimore Bullets, a brand-new team, won the BAA championship in 1948 behind the fine play of Buddy Jeannette, a basketball gypsy who starred for many teams during the 1930s and 40s. By all accounts, the 1948 NBL champions, Minneapolis Lakers, led by Mikan and Jim Pollard, were a far superior team.

The BAA finally got smart and realized the best way to beat the NBL was to swallow it. The upstart league lured four of the NBL's best franchises—the Rochester Royals, Fort Wayne Pistons, Indianapolis Jets, and powerhouse Minneapolis Lakers—into its fold with the promise of huge crowds and big gate receipts. Of these franchises, three are still in the NBA today, although none of them in their original home city. More importantly, in one fell swoop, the BAA added Mikan, Pollard, Arnie Ferrin, Bob Davies, Arnie Risen, Bobby Wanzer, Ray Lumpp, and Red Holzman to its marquee. All of these men were among the game's elite. Minneapolis and Rochester dominated in their first BAA season, going a combined 89-31 against the rest of the clubs. Mikan and the Lakers destroyed the Washington Capitols in the 1949 finals.

Prior to the 1949-50 season, the BAA achieved its dream of owning all of the nation's top pro basketball talent. The NBL saw the writing on the wall and accepted the BAA's offer to merge. The new league, which started with 17 teams, was renamed the National Basketball Association. Every team joined the new NBA, including the Redskins from tiny Sheboygan, Wisconsin, and the Rockets from far-flung Denver. There was little chance that so many teams could prosper financially, but league officials were just happy to have peace in pro basketball. They figured some teams would move or fold or join forces, but no one expected the smaller clubs to survive.

The inaugural NBA finals—the first true championship of professional basketball—were held at the conclusion of the 1949-50 season, between the Minneapolis Lakers and the Syracuse Nationals.

CHAPTER 1

THE 1950s

1950
Syracuse Nationals vs. Minneapolis Lakers

The Minneapolis Lakers, coached by Johnny Kundla, were a bruising bunch led by center George Mikan, the league's top scorer and most dominating presence in the paint. Though his glasses made him look like Clark Kent, the 6'10" Mikan played like Superman. Joining him on the front line were forwards Jim Pollard and Vern Mikkelsen, neither of whom was afraid to mix it up. In the backcourt, Herm Schaefer and Slater Martin were steady ballhandlers and hard-nosed defenders. No one doubted that the Lakers were battle-tested. After finishing in a tie for first place in the Central Division at 51-17 with the Rochester Royals, they won a one-game tiebreaker to christen their playoff run. Minneapolis then defeated the Chicago Stags, Fort Wayne Pistons, and Anderson Duffy Packers without a loss to advance to the NBA Finals. With Mikan netting more than 30 points a game in the post-season, the Lakers were confident they could handle any opponent.

Syracuse had just as much reason to feel good about its chances. The Nationals were a more balanced team than Minneapolis,

George Mikan powers his way to two points with a left-handed hook. Mikan was the dominant player in the early days of pro basketball.

featuring eight players who could contribute on offense. Head coach Al Cervi, who also served as the team's point guard, saw this as a distinct advantage. During the regular season, Syracuse beat up the competition, posting a league-best record of 51-13 on its way to the Eastern Division crown. The heart of the team was Cervi and guard Paul Seymour, whose physical style always sparked his teammates. The soul was Dolph Schayes, a muscular forward who could do it all. Flanked by Alex Hannum and George Ratkovicz, Schayes seemed to have more than enough brawn on either side of him to neutralize Mikan. After defeating the Philadelphia Warriors in their first playoff series, the Nationals edged out the New York Knickerbockers to earn a shot at the title.

The best-of-seven series opened at the State Fair Coliseum in Syracuse, New York, where the Nationals had posted a 34-1 record during the regular season and playoffs. Minneapolis, however, was not intimidated. Feeding the ball to Mikan time and again, the Lakers stayed close throughout the game and were within a basket as the clock wound down. Bud Grant, a Minneapolis sub who years later would go on to coach the NFL's Minnesota Vikings, knotted the score with a hook shot, then Mikan knocked away a layup attempt by Cervi. A rookie named Bob "Tiger" Harrison pounced on the loose ball for the Lakers and canned a 40-footer at the buzzer to give his team a dramatic 68-66 victory. The next night the Nationals discovered Mikan's kryptonite: he was allergic to smoke. The haze of cigar and cigarette smoke that typically hung over the court in the dank, poorly ventilated arenas of the day dropped down for some reason, and the big man had trouble seeing and breathing. The Nats knot-

ted the best-of-seven series at 1-1 with a 91-85 win.

The stage shifted to Minnesota for Game 3, and the Lakers took control. With Mikan, Pollard, and Mikkelsen throwing hips and elbows, Minneapolis bullied its way to a pair of victories, 91-77 and 77-69. With their backs against the wall, the Nationals returned home armed with a new strategy. Cervi assigned the job of covering Pollard to Seymour, and the pesky guard held the big forward to six points in an 83-76 triumph. The series returned to Minnesota, where the Lakers decided to fight fire with fire. Playing with renewed ferocity, they manhandled the Nationals. Mikan was unstoppable, scoring 40 points, while his teammates greeted every push from Syracuse with a harder shove of their own. Though four Lakers fouled out, Minneapolis cruised 110-95 to claim the first NBA championship. Today's fans would have found the brutal style of this series appalling, but that's the way they played in the early years of the NBA.

Lakers 4
Nationals 2
Best Player: George Mikan, Minneapolis

1951
New York Knickerbockers vs. Rochester Royals

Heading into the 1951 playoffs, it seemed that the Minneapolis Lakers were primed to defend their crown. But two things worked against them. First, the league had whittled itself down from 17 teams to 11. The remaining teams were deeper and more talented. Second, George Mikan injured his ankle, removing the one great advantage the Lakers lorded over the rest of the league. The team that stood to gain the most from these developments was the Rochester Royals. Coached by Les Harrison, the Royals had been a perennial title contender since the late 1940s. But Minneapolis usually gave Rochester fits, especially with Mikan in the middle. With Big George hurting, however, Harrison's troops had the edge. The Royals were built on speed and guile in the backcourt. Guard Bob Davies, the team's unquestioned leader, confounded opponents—and sometimes his own teammates—with an array of no-look passes. His running mate was Bobby Wanzer, also a talented offensive player. The muscle was provided by center Arnie Risen and forwards Jack Coleman and Arnie Johnson. After Minneapolis's frontcourt, this trio was the toughest in the league. Off the bench, Harrison relied on an athletic forward named Bill Calhoun and Red Holzman, a guard with a real head for the game. After finishing as the runner-up to the Lakers in the Western Division, Rochester beat the Fort Wayne Pistons in the first round of the playoffs, setting up a duel with the Lakers in a best-of-five semi-final series. The Royals dropped the first game, but charged back to take the next three and moved on to the finals.

Their opponent, the New York Knickerbockers, also hailed from the Empire State. That the Knicks were this close to an NBA title was news in and of itself. Joe Lapchick's crew had finished the regular season at an unspectacular 36-30 in the Eastern Division. New York, however, jelled at precisely the right time. With heralded playmaker Dick McGuire running the show at the point, the Knicks stormed past the Boston Celtics in the

first round. McGuire's partner in the backcourt, Max Zaslofsky, played brilliantly. So did New York's three frontcourt stars. Forward Vince Boryla scored at will against Boston, and Harry Gallatin, the league's most dynamic rebounder, controlled the boards. He got help from center Nat "Sweetwater" Clifton, a powerful 6'6" center. A former member of the Harlem Globetrotters, Clifton had joined the Knicks just before the season began. In fact, he and Chuck Cooper of the Celtics were the first two black African Americans to play in the NBA. After handling Boston, New York faced the Syracuse

Max Zaslofsky, the masterful backcourt star of the Knicks and Pistons. His teams made the NBA finals five times between 1951 and 1956.

Nationals. In a topsy-turvy series, the Knicks emerged victorious in Game 5, giving them an unlikely shot at championship glory.

The finals match-up between the Royals and Knicks created a buzz throughout New York. Early on, however, Rochester brought the Knicks and their fans back to earth with an awesome display of speed and strength. At home to start the series in Edgerton Park Sports Arena (where New York had not won in 3 years), the Royals pasted their cross-state rivals twice, 92-65 and 99-84. Davies starred in both contests, completely outplaying McGuire. In Game 3 at New York's 69th Regiment Armory, Risen stepped up, netting 27 points in a 78-71 win. Rochester

Boston's "Easy" Ed Macauley grabs a rebound against the Knicks. The All-Star center failed to click with Bob Cousy, but was traded for someone who did—Bill Russell.

was now in total command. When the Knicks blew a 17-point lead and then fell behind by 6 points late in Game 4, the series appeared to be over. But Clifton led a furious rally that sparked the Knicks to a 79-73 victory. New York then broke its jinx in Rochester, defeating the Royals 92-89. Back home in Madison Square Garden, the Knicks won Game 6, 80-73, as Zaslofsky poured in 23 points.

The tension for the final game of the series was thick. Rochester surged to an early lead, but New York battled back and trailed by only 6 points at the half. In the fourth quarter, the Knicks first tied the contest, and then moved ahead on a lay-up by Gallatin. Moments later, Clifton was whistled for his sixth foul, opening up room for Risen down low. When he connected on a hook shot and a free throw, the Royals regained the lead, 75-74. Davies sank a pair of free throws to extend Rochester's advantage, then Holzman dribbled out the clock moments later before feeding Coleman for a final basket to make it 79-75. The Royals were NBA champs, but they had nearly blown a 3 game to 0 lead.

> Royals 4
> Knicks 3
> **Best Player: Bob Davies, Rochester**

1952
New York Knickerbockers vs. Minneapolis Lakers

His ankle healed, George Mikan entered the 1951-52 season determined to reclaim the NBA crown for Minneapolis. The league had instituted a new rule, however, which threatened to neutralize the Lakers' inside advantage. By widening the three-second lane from 6 feet to 12 feet, NBA officials hoped to spread the floor and open the game for smaller players, which would boost scoring. While this is exactly what happened, Mikan and feisty forwards Jim Pollard and Vern Mikkelsen also found more room to maneuver, and the trio remained the league's most fearsome frontcourt combos.

Coach Johnny Kundla knew Minneapolis also needed a threat from the outside to compliment his team's power in the pivot. With the reliable Slater Martin still at the point, Kundla tried Whitey Skoog at the other guard. When he went down with a knee injury, the coach turned to Pep Saul, whom the Lakers had acquired from the Baltimore Bullets. As fate would have it, Saul's deadly accurate two-handed set shot proved the key ingredient to Minneapolis' championship mix. After finishing second with a 40-26 record to the Rochester Royals in the Western Division, the Lakers breezed past the Indianapolis Olympians and destroyed the defending champion Royals to earn a berth in the finals.

In the Eastern Division, the New York Knickerbockers hoped to rekindle the fire of their improbable run the year before. The team's cast of characters was virtually unchanged, though Connie Simmons replaced Sweetwater Clifton in the starting lineup at center. Vince Boryla and Harry Gallatin filled out the forward line, while the backcourt featured Dick McGuire and Max Zaslofsky again. Coach Joe Lapchick continued to use the players on his bench liberally, with Clifton and Ernie Vandeweghe logging plenty of minutes. When a knee injury sidelined Boryla, Vandeweghe took his place upfront, and New York never skipped a beat. The Knicks ended the regular season at 37-29, just behind the Syracuse Nationals and Boston Celtics.

Jim Pollard splits the Rochester defense for a layup. Known as "Jumping Jim" and the "Kangaroo Kid," Pollard entertained teammates with slam dunks in practice, but never tried one during a game.

They surprised Bob Cousy and the run-and-gun Celts in the first round and upended the talent-laden Nats in the second.

In the first quarter of the opener, Dick McGuire's brother, Al, hit a running layup and was fouled during the shot, but neither official saw the ball go in. Though Lapchick complained bitterly, the basket was ignored. The oversight came back to haunt the visiting New Yorkers when the contest went into overtime tied at 71-71. In the extra period, Pollard sunk four crucial free throws for an 83-79 victory. Minneapolis lost the following night, as the Knicks did a great job defending against

The appeal of big-time basketball has always translated into selling power. Long before Michael Jordan was pushing Nikes and Gatorade, George Mikan was endorsing Pro Keds.

in check all night long. With Zaslofsky exploding for the 17 points in the second half, New York cruised 76-68 and pushed the Lakers to the brink. The bad news for the Knicks was that Game 7 would be played in the Minneapolis Auditorium. Brimming with confidence, the Lakers controlled the contest from the opening tap. Thanks to another big effort from Mikan, Minneapolis won easily and brought the NBA title back to Minnesota.

Lakers 4
Knicks 3
Best Player: George Mikan, Minneapolis

1953
New York Knickerbockers vs. Minneapolis Lakers

As the NBA grew in popularity, the advantage of playing before a raucous hometown crowd was becoming ever greater. Minneapolis certainly saw it that way. The Lakers had captured their second NBA crown in 1952 partly because they hosted Game 7. To seize the homecourt edge again throughout the postseason, they knew they had to post the league's best record in the regular season. Though George Mikan's scoring average dropped to just over 20 points a night, he led the NBA in rebounding for the second year in a row. Jim Pollard and Vern Mikkelsen gave coach Johnny Kundla their usual fine efforts, and Slater Martin and Pep Saul settled in comfortably with each other in the backcourt. The Lakers charged to a record of 48-22, clinching precious homecourt advantage. In the playoffs, they quickly disposed of the Indianapolis Olympians and then fought off the Fort Wayne Pistons.

Mikan, Pollard, and Mikkelsen. The Lakers regained their form in New York's 69th Regiment Armory, seizing an 82-77 win. In Game 4, the series appeared to shift in favor of the Knicks when Pollard hurt his back and was forced to the sidelines. The injury allowed New York to focus all its defensive energy on Mikan, and the home team won 90-89 in overtime.

Back in Minnesota for Game 5, the Lakers found their rhythm with reserve Bob Harrison replacing Pollard. Mikan and Mikkelsen each scored 32 points, and Saul added 15, sparking Minneapolis to an easy 102-89 victory. Given up for dead, the Knicks responded with a suffocating effort in Game 6, holding the Lakers

Slater Martin pushes the ball down the court. The Minneapolis point guard's job was to feed the ball to the Laker front line.

more Bullets and followed up that performance with an equally impressive series win over the Boston Celtics.

To have a chance against the mighty Lakers, the Knicks figured they would have to take one of the first two contests in Minnesota. In Game 1, they stayed close for the first three quarters before shocking Minneapolis with a 30-point outburst in the final period and streaking to a 96-88 victory. The Lakers started Game 2 on a tear, building a 17-point lead by halftime. Though the Knicks battled back, Minneapolis held on to win 73-71 in a game that was decided on the foul line. Minneapolis took Game 3 by a score of 90-75 after Mikan scrapped a turn-

The New York Knickerbockers also broke from the gate quickly and ran neck-and-neck with the Lakers all year for the league's best regular-season record. Despite an injury to Max Zaslofsky, coach Joe Lapchick still had a varied arsenal of offensive weapons. Sweetwater Clifton was the starter at center again, flanked as usual by Vince Boryla and Harry Gallatin. In the backcourt, Dick McGuire remained a steady presence, while newcomer Carl Braun took over for Zaslofsky. Ernie Vandeweghe and Connie Simmons provided clutch scoring and strong rebounding off the bench. New York finished 47-23, a game worse than the Minneapolis game. The Knicks then sizzled in their opening round sweep of the Balti-

George Mikan celebrates with teammates after scoring 48 points against the Knicks in a regular-season game. He was equally tough in the playoffs, leading the Lakers to victory over New York in the 1952 and '53 finals.

TEAM SPIRIT
1950s: MINNEAPOLIS LAKERS

In each decade, there has been an NBA champion that truly embodied the spirit of the game during that era. Some dominated their opponents, winning multiple titles, while others just won a couple. Each club, however, played an important role in the evolution of basketball. As their opponents developed new strategies and nurtured new talent in order to beat these great teams, the sport itself changed and grew in amazing ways.

The first team to set the bar high was the Minneapolis Lakers. Originally a member of the old National Basketball League, the Lakers competed in world championship exhibition tournaments against other pro clubs in the 1940s and dominated the opposition. When they abandoned the NBL and joined the fledgling Basketball Association of America in 1948, it was perhaps the key development of the pre-NBA era.

The Lakers perfected the brand of hard-nosed basketball played in the late 1940s and early 1950s. In the days before there was a shot clock, teams pounded away at each other with hips, knees, and elbows, and ran one set play after another in an attempt to trick opponents or just wear them down. It was not a very pretty game, and it was played far below the rim.

The Lakers fielded a team that was perfect for the demands of slow-down basketball. Their bespectacled center, George Mikan, was a giant of his time, standing 6'10". Mikan would establish position on a defender, receive a pass, and then back his man into the basket until he could turn around a toss in a short shot. Anyone who tried to swipe the ball from "Big George" was in danger of losing their front teeth. Anyone who stood up to him was pummeled like a prize fighter.

around jumper he had been working on and dominated the second half. The next night, in another contest bogged down by fouls, the Lakers won as Gallatin missed a hook shot at the buzzer for New York.

Coach Kundla rewarded his team with a day off, and they painted the town red before heading back to Minnesota, hopping from nightclub to nightclub in the Big Apple. Predictably, after a hot start, the Lakers ran out of gas in the second half of Game 5,

and the Knicks mounted a comeback charge. With their lead cut to a basket in the fourth quarter, the Lakers stirred from their slumber and won 91-84 with some clutch free throws in the closing minutes.

Lakers 4
Knicks 1
Best Player: George Mikan, Minneapolis

Just in case opponents decided to gang up on Mikan, the Lakers had a pair of outstanding wingmen to make them pay. Vern Mikkelson, a star pivot player in college, made a great adjustment to his new role and practically invented the position of power forward. He specialized in putting back Mikan's misses and could also shoot from medium range with a two-handed, overhead set shot. His counterpart, Jim Pollard, was a forward who could run the floor, dribble and pass like a guard, and shoot the jump shot, which was still something of a novelty when he broke into the NBA. At 6'5", he did not exactly tower over defenders, but he was one of the few pros who could dunk the ball.

The Minneapolis guards were responsible for feeding the ball to the Lakers' front line. Slater Martin, a 5'10" playmaker who could also score when he was needed, ran the offense from the point and harassed enemy guards on defense. The other guard slot was filled by a number of different role players, including Whitey Skoog, Bob Harrison, Pep Saul, Swede Carlson, Herm Schaefer, and Arnie Ferrin, who also subbed for Mikkelson and Pollard.

Under coach Johnny Kundla, the Lakers won the NBL title in 1948, the BAA title in 1949, and were NBA champions in 1950, 1952, 1953, and 1954. Minneapolis was so dominant that many teams chose to simply hold the ball on offense rather than giving Mikan and his accomplices a chance to get it back. The NBA, fearing this would drive crowds away from its games, instituted the 24-second clock after the Lakers won the championship in 1954. This transformed basketball, as it took the advantage away from players like Mikan and shone the spotlight on versatile performers who could create their own shots.

1954
Syracuse Nationals vs. Minneapolis Lakers

Though the NBA secured its first television contract during the 1953-54 campaign, all was not well with the league. Financial woes and scandal forced the Indianapolis Olympians to cease operations, reducing the number of teams in the league to nine. The game itself was suffering, too. Play had become so physical that games often degenerated into whistle-blowing foul fests. Of course, this rough-and-tumble style played right into the hands of the Minneapolis Lakers. With George Mikan still in his prime, the defending champs looked nearly unbeatable. Jim Pollard, Vern Mikkelsen, and Slater Martin returned, and coach Johnny Kundla tabbed Whitey Skoog as his fifth starter. With Pep Saul coming off the bench and heralded rookie Clyde Lovellette

GEORGE MIKAN
CENTER, MINNEAPOLIS LAKERS

JIM POLLARD
FORWARD, MINNEAPOLIS LAKERS

These cards of George Mikan and Jim Pollard, cut from the back of a Wheaties box in the early 1950s, are among the oldest and rarest from the early days of the NBA. Mikan, Pollard, and Rochester star Bob Davies were the only basketball players in the cereal company's 40-card set.

spelling Big George when needed, the Lakers enjoyed tremendous depth, which they used to go 46-26 and win the Western Division. In the playoffs, Minneapolis handled the Fort Wayne Pistons and Rochester Royals with ease to advance to the finals for the third year in a row.

The Syracuse Nationals also were masters in the NBA's hand-to-hand combat. Since their trip to the championship series in 1951, however, Al Cervi's troops had experienced nothing but frustration in the postseason. This year, despite the absence of a true center, the Nats hoped to reverse that trend. With Dolph Schayes and workmanlike Earl Lloyd sharing responsibilities in the middle, Syracuse tied for second in the Eastern Division at 42-30. Schayes

topped the team in scoring and rebounding, getting help up front from forward Wally Osterkorn. The tandem of Paul Seymour and George King at guard was solid. The Nationals' road to the finals wasn't easy. In overcoming the Knicks and Celtics, Seymour fractured a thumb, and Schayes and Lloyd each suffered a broken hand.

Most experts expected the Lakers to manhandle the battered Nats. Game 1 went according to this script, as Minneapolis rolled to a 79-68 win. But Syracuse came out hungry the next night. Up by 10 points in the fourth quarter, the Nationals lost another key player when King broke a wrist after a hard foul by Mikan. After the Lakers charged back to knot the contest at 60-60, Seymour dribbled upcourt with the clock winding down. Rather than driving to the hoop, he surprised everyone by launching a set shot from 43 feet. When the bomb swished, the Laker crowd sat in stunned silenced.

The teams split the following two games in Syracuse, but bad luck struck the home team yet again when reserve Billy Gabor was sidelined with a knee injury. Minneapolis revisited a familiar strategy in Game 5, pounding the ball down low to Mikan and Pollard, who bullied their way to the basket time and again in an 84-73 victory. That set the stage for what fans in Minnesota assumed would be an easy end to a difficult series. The Nats, however, didn't cooperate. With time running out, Syracuse had possession with the score tied 63-63. The ball found its way to backup center Jim Neal, who heaved it up from 27 feet. It went right through for another miracle victory—this one forcing a seventh game. The experienced Lakers took the defeat in stride. They opened Game 7 calm and composed and flattened the Nationals 87-80, thanks in part to 21 points from Pollard. Afterwards, Mikan quietly retired, more than satisfied with his team's fourth NBA title.

> Lakers 4
> Nationals 3
> Best Player: George Mikan, Minneapolis

1955
Syracuse Nationals vs. Fort Wayne Pistons

The NBA had a completely revamped look in 1954-55. Danny Biasone, part owner of the Syracuse Nationals, hated the plodding, hacking style of basketball most teams em-

ployed. He convinced the league to adopt a 24-second shot clock. Biasone correctly reasoned that this would increase scoring by forcing teams to shoot more often and also place greater emphasis on the athleticism of the league's top stars.

No team benefited more from the new rule than his Nats. Coach Al Cervi's bunch boasted skilled players at several key positions, including Dolph Schayes at forward, Paul Seymour and George King in the backcourt, and Johnny Kerr and Connie Simmons off the bench. With Earl Lloyd and Red Rocha willing to do the dirty work down low, Syracuse was a team full of "go-to guys" who could create their own shots. The Nats surged to the Eastern Division

Long before Larry, Magic, and Michael "saved" basketball, innovator Danny Biasone left his mark on the game. His idea for a 24-second shot clock quickened the pace of NBA action.

crown with a record of 43-29. After a bye in the first round of the playoffs, they faced off against the Boston Celtics, beating them handily in four games.

The Fort Wayne Pistons also liked the new pace. Under the guidance of first-year coach Charley Eckman, Fort Wayne dethroned the Minneapolis Lakers—minus George Mikan— in the Western Division. The team's strength was its powerful, savvy front line made up of George Yardley, Mel Hutchins, and Larry Foust. Clutch performers Andy Phillip and Max Zaslofsky, the former New York Knick, teamed up to give the Pistons veteran leadership and reliable scoring in the backcourt. Backing them up was guard Frankie Brian, an All-Star in his earlier days. Fort Wayne outran the compe-

George Yardley, the "go-to" guy of the Pistons. Yardley was the top scorer on Ft. Wayne's powerful front line.

tition in the West, posting a 43-29 record. In the postseason, the Pistons ended the Lakers' string of 3 titles, eliminating the defending champs in 4 games.

The finals opened in Syracuse with Fort Wayne looking to grab the momentum. Simmons, who injured his back during the season, was not available for action. The 22-year-old Kerr was playing in his place. With the Nats trailing by 4 in the 4th quarter, however, Cervi inserted reserve Dick Farley. The little-used guard provided a huge spark, rallying Syracuse to an 86-82 comeback victory. The Nationals rode that wave into Game 2, as Schayes scored 24 points and Rocha canned a big shot to secure an 87-84 win. Playing before its supportive home fans, Fort Wayne took the next two. Hutchins starred in Game 3, scoring 22 points and controlling the boards. The following game, the Pistons stepped up the defensive pressure and limited Syracuse to just 32 of 103 shots from the field. Game 5 proved the most bizarre of the series. Down by 15 points, the Nats stormed back in the second half, only to have their momentum disrupted when a fan tossed his folding chair on the court. When play resumed, the Pistons regained their composure and won 74-71.

Now it was the Nationals looking to turn the series around. Lifting their spirits was their return to the Syracuse War Memorial, where Fort Wayne had not won in six seasons. Early on, the Pistons were on course to end the jinx, but the action was halted when a fight erupted between Fort Wayne's Don Meineke and Syracuse's Wally Osterkorn. The inspired Nats then battled back to capture an emotional 109-104 victory. Game 7 also started on a tense note, and Syracuse fans became even more concerned when the Pistons built a 17-point lead. But Farley and another reserve, Billy Kenville, spearheaded a charge that enabled the Nats to tie the score at 91-91. King then got fouled and converted on 1 of 2 from the line. When Seymour knocked away Fort Wayne's inbound pass, Syracuse held on for its first title.

Nationals 4
Pistons 3
Best Player: Dolph Schayes, Syracuse

1956
Philadelphia Warriors vs. Fort Wayne Pistons

For years, the Philadelphia Warriors had languished in or near the basement of the Eastern Division. Then came Tom Gola, and the team's fortunes changed. A 6'6" All-American center in college, the rookie made the switch to guard in the NBA and became an instant star. Paired with Jack George in Philadelphia's backcourt, he filled out half of the biggest guard tandem in the league.

Dolph Schayes takes it to the hole against Bill Russell. The fearless and talented Schayes led Syracuse to the 1955 NBA championship.

Center Neil Johnston outmuscles two Knicks for a rebound. The Philadelphia center was an unstoppable force around the basket.

Explosive scorers Paul Arizin and Neil Johnston joined enforcer Joe Graboski on the forward line, giving the Warriors a perfect mixture of players for the pro game's new, up-tempo style. Philadelphia soared to the top of the East standings a year after the team had finished dead last. Arizin and Johnston each averaged more than 20 points a game, while Gola provided size and strength never seen before in a guard. In the playoffs, the Warriors won a wild series against the Syracuse Nationals, beating the defending champs to move on to the finals.

The Fort Wayne Pistons had a fight on their hands, too. Coach Charley Eckman piloted his squad to first place in the Western Division, relying once again on the trio of George Yardley, Mel Hutchins, and Larry Foust—who together averaged nearly 50 points and more than 30 rebounds a game. Chuck Noble replaced Max Zaslofsky in the starting backcourt beside Andy Phillip, while Bobby Houbregs, Walter Devlin, and Marion Spears excelled in supporting roles. The Pistons finished first in a weak Western Division with a 37-35 record, then had to fend off a spirited challenge from the improving St. Louis Hawks team to advance to the championship round.

On the strength of its record in the regular season, Philadelphia claimed the home-court advantage in the finals. In Game 1, the Pistons dug in on defense, building a 15-point lead in the second quarter. Coach George Senesky gambled with reserve Ernie Beck, who caught fire from the field. By the start of the fourth quarter, the Warriors were ahead comfortably and won 98-94. The series shifted to Fort Wayne for Game 2, and the Pistons evened things up with an 84-83 victory, as Yardley hit several late clutch free throws. Philadelphia returned home to a

jam-packed Conventions Hall for the next contest. Arizin netted 27 points and the Warriors scored a 100-96 win.

For Game 4, both teams traveled back to Fort Wayne, where Philly had never enjoyed much success. But Arizin was unstoppable again, pouring in 30 points, while Gola added 19. Though the Pistons mounted a late rally, the Warriors hung on 107-105 to seize command of the series. They proceeded to wrap it up in Game 5, treating their hometown fans to a 99-88 victory. The win capped one of the most amazing turnarounds in NBA history, as the Warriors rode Arizin's hot-shooting and Gola's steady play to go from worst to first.

Warriors 4
Pistons 1
Best Player: Paul Arizin, Philadelphia

1957
Boston Celtics vs. St. Louis Hawks

When Red Auerbach took over the Boston Celtics as coach and general manager in 1950, he was asked to revitalize the struggling franchise. His first move—one in a career of shrewd moves—was to draft Bob Cousy, the ballhandling wizard out of Holy Cross. Auerbach then built a team around Cousy, adding players with varied offensive skills who would thrive alongside the "Houdini of the Hardwood."

Boston made the playoffs most years but failed to find a championship formula. Auerbach realized that he needed a pivot man who could defend, rebound, and run the floor. He thought Ed Macauley might be his man, but

Bob Cousy redefined the point guard position, but it was not until Bill Russell joined the team that the Celtics became an NBA powerhouse.

the center never clicked with Cousy. Finally, in the spring of 1956, the Boston coach got his man: Bill Russell. It cost the Celtics Macauley and forward Cliff Hagan, who were shipped to the St. Louis Hawks for the No. 2 pick in the draft. With the first pick, the Royals selected Si Green of Duquesne, and Boston grabbed Russell, who had starred for the University of San Francisco.

Russell spent the first part of the 1956-57 campaign playing for the U.S. Olympic team, which won a gold medal in Melbourne, Australia. When he finally joined the Celtics, it was obvious that Auerbach had found exactly what he was after. Cousy, the league's best passer, and Russell, the league's best rebounder and defender, were

TWO-MAN GAME
BOB COUSY AND BILL RUSSELL

Bob Cousy had already put together quite a resumé before Bill Russell joined the Celtics during the 1956-57 season. The team's longtime point guard had revolutionized the game with his fancy dribbling and passing and was working on a fifth straight assist title when the rookie center from the University of San Francisco joined the club 24 games into the year. But from the first night these two men played together, the Celtics were a completely different team. Indeed, over the next seven years, Cousy and Russell reached the NBA Finals an amazing seven times. Prior to their pairing, the Celtics had never played for the league championship.

Never before had a guard and center worked so well together. When Russell pulled down a defensive rebound, he knew exactly where Cousy would be to receive the outlet pass. The lightning-quick pivot man would fire the ball to his teammate, who would then turn upcourt and look for another Celtic streaking toward the enemy basket. This two-man game terrorized opponents to such a degree that they sometimes retreated as soon as they shot. Even when they got back in time to cover all the Celtic forwards and guards, however. Russell often out-sprinted the enemy center to receive a return pass from Cousy to finish the play he started with a thundering dunk.

perfect together. Assembled around them were several lethal scorers, including sweet-shooting guard Bill Sharman and rookie forward Tom Heinsohn, as well as experienced vets like Andy Phillip and Jim Loscutoff. Boston raced to a 44-28 record in the regular season, tops in the NBA. The Celtics then dispatched the Syracuse Nationals in 3 games to get their first shot at an NBA title.

Their opponent in the finals, St. Louis, offered several familiar faces, as Macauley started at forward and Hagan came off the bench to log important minutes. But coach Alex Hannum's most dangerous weapon was Bob Pettit, a versatile forward who was all but unguardable. With the cagey Slater Martin and Jack McMahon in the backcourt, and dependable Jack Coleman up front, the Hawks developed into a menacing team come the playoffs. Although they finished with an unimpressive 34-38 record, it was good enough for a three-way, first-place tie with the Pistons and Lakers in the rebuilding Western Division. St. Louis beat both clubs in tie-breaking contests to earn a bye to the conference finals, then swept the Lakers in three straight— including a 143-135 double-overtime thriller—to set up a showdown with the Celtics.

The finals started much like the previous series had ended for the Hawks. Though the Celts were heavily favored on the parquet floor of the Boston Garden, St. Louis stole Game 1 by a score of 125-123 when Coleman hit a long shot with time running out in the second overtime. In the next contest, Boston was determined to stop Pettit, who had hit for 37 points in the previous game. When Russell and his teammates accomplished their mission, the Celtics walked away with an easy 119-99 victory. In St. Louis for the next two games, the Hawks

looked to their notoriously rough crowd to unnerve Boston. They got what they wanted in Game 3, as the Celtics played tentatively. With the score tied at 98-98 late in the fourth quarter, Pettit came up big again, nailing an outside shot for the win. In Game 4, Cousy took control, shooting and passing Boston to a 5-point win that evened the series.

The Celtics returned home for the next game and rolled again, blowing out the Hawks 124-109. When the series moved

Bob Pettit lays one in for the Hawks. The wiry 6' 9" forward could score from anywhere and was a dominant rebounder.

back to St. Louis for Game 6, the Hawks focused their defensive efforts on Cousy with tremendous results. The exhausted point guard stepped to the foul line with a chance to put his team ahead with 12 seconds left, but missed both attempts. St. Louis then rushed the ball downcourt and fed Pettit, whose shot rolled out. Hagan, however, was positioned perfectly for the tip-in, and the Hawks survived 96-94.

That victory set the stage for a classic Game 7. The lead seesawed back and forth until late in the fourth quarter. With his team down 101-100, Russell blocked a shot and scored at the other end. Moments later Pettit calmly sank two free throws to send the contest to OT. The Celtics appeared to have the game in hand, but Coleman canned another jumper to tie things up at the end of the first period. In the second overtime, Loscutoff converted two from the line to put Boston ahead 125-123. When the Hawks failed in a desperation attempt to knot the score, the Celtics were champs. "The first one is always the hardest," said Auerbach years later. "It's also the most satisfying."

Celtics 4
Hawks 3
Best Player: Bill Russell, Boston

1958
Boston Celtics vs. St. Louis Hawks

The St. Louis Hawks were a hungry team. Coach Alex Hannum was blessed with the most versatile front line in basketball, with the incomparable Bob Pettit, Cliff Hagan, a second-year player on the verge of greatness, and the cagey veteran Ed Macauley. In the backcourt, Slater Martin and Jack McMahon committed few errors and were content to feed the big guys. Off the bench, Jack Coleman, Chuck Share, and Win Wilfong were consistent performers. The Hawks took the Western Division by storm in the regular season, finishing in first by eight games, then advanced to the finals for the second year in a row, defeating the Detroit Pistons 4 games to 1.

Standing in the Hawks' way was an opponent they knew all too well. Boston was fast becoming the NBA's glamour franchise.

Cliff Hagan drops in two against the Celtics. The St. Louis forward, better known for his hook shot, was part of the Hawks' formidable front line.

Just as coach Red Auerbach had envisioned, Bill Russell and Bob Cousy provided a maddening mixture of defense and offense that was nearly impossible to match. High-scoring guard Bill Sharman and energetic forward Tom Heinsohn were ideal complements, both able to hit the open shots they were so often afforded. Lou Tsioropoulos instead of Jim Loscutoff, out for the season due to illness, rounded out the starting five. However, sixth-man Frank Ramsey had the easier name to pronounce and was always in at crunch time. Auerbach's troops dominated the Eastern Division, posting a record of 49-23. In the playoffs, they handled the Philadelphia Warriors with relative ease, taking the series 4 games to 1.

Boston again held homecourt advantage, and St. Louis again rendered it meaningless with a 104-102 shocker in Game 1. The Celtics responded like champs in the next contest, embarrassing the Hawks 136-112. Then came the turning point of the finals. Russell injured his ankle midway through Game 3, and would not return for the rest of the post-season. Without their imposing shot blocker and rebounder, the Celtics were forced to play into the Hawks' hands. St. Louis cruised to a 111-108 victory to grab a 2 games to 1 series lead.

The gritty Celtics refused to go down without a fight. Calling on subs Arnie Risen and Jack Nichols to fill in for Russell, they surprised the Hawks by winning Game 4. Then in the friendly confines of the Boston Garden they battled St. Louis to the bitter end in Game 5, only to fall in a 102-100 heartbreaker. Back at the Kiel Auditorium for Game 6, the Hawks knew they had to put the Celtics away. Pettit led the charge. Through the first three quarters, he had 31 points, but Boston kept the score close. In the final period, "Big Blue," as he was known to the St. Louis faithful, staged one of the greatest performances in NBA history. Connecting from everywhere on the floor, he netted 19 of the last 21 points scored by the Hawks. His final bucket, a follow-up of a missed shot, secured his team's 110-109 victory. On the strength of Pettit's awesome 50-point performance, St. Louis had dethroned Boston for the title.

> Hawks 4
> Celtics 2
> Best Player: Bob Pettit, St. Louis

1959
Boston Celtics vs. Minneapolis Lakers

After being derailed by the St. Louis Hawks, the Boston Celtics were eager to return to the summit of pro basketball. There was no reason to believe the team wouldn't do just that. Russell had recovered from his ankle injury and, with Bob Cousy and Bill Sharman in the backcourt, gave coach Red Auerbach three All-Stars. Tom Heinsohn continued to improve, while Jim Loscutoff was back at full health. Reserve guards Frank Ramsey and Sam Jones would have started for most other teams, while rookie K.C. Jones added further depth. Boston again waltzed through the regular season, winning the Eastern Division easily with a record of 52-20. In the playoffs, the Celtics faced their staunchest challenge from the Syracuse Nationals. The home team won every game in this taut, best-of-seven series, with Boston capturing the finale on their distinctive parquet floor.

The Western Division's representative in the finals was the Minneapolis Lakers. After languishing without George Mikan, they discovered a one-man rebuilding project named Elgin Baylor. The 6'5" rookie forward was built like a football linebacker but had the grace, dexterity and leaping ability

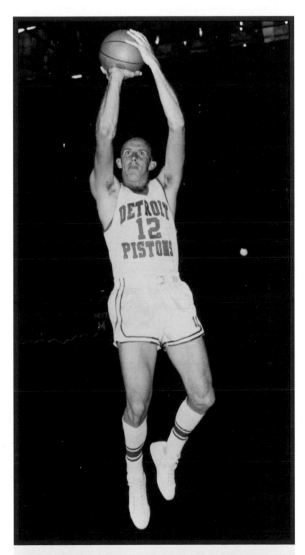

George Yardley could score from anywhere on the floor. He shattered the NBA record for points in a season in 1955-56, but his Pistons fell again in the finals.

of a ballet dancer. Baylor could launch his jumper directly over an opponent and drive around all but the very best defenders in the league. He also happened to be a superb rebounder. Baylor headed an experienced squad that included Vern Mikkelsen, Larry Foust, Dick Garmaker, Slick Leonard, and Hot Rod Hundley. The Lakers finished 33-39 under coach Johnny Kundla but caught fire in the post-season. First, Minneapolis beat the Detroit Pistons in a best-of-three series. Then Kundla's troops upset the St. Louis Hawks to move on to the finals.

On paper, the championship series appeared to be an awful mismatch. Over the past two seasons, the Celtics had defeated the Lakers in 18 straight, including a 173-139 blowout two months before. On the hardwood, things played out pretty much as expected. Boston swept the first two games at home by scores of 118-115 and 128-108. No one could keep Russell off the boards, Cousy ran the fast break like a conquering general, and super sub Ramsey was among the team's leading scorers. When the action shifted to Minnesota, the Celtics continued to roll. They took Game 3 by a score of 123-110, and then completed the job in Game 4, 118-113. Boston's annihilation of the Lakers marked the first sweep in NBA finals history. The fact that three of the four games were tightly contested led many basketball fans to predict that the Celtics would be vulnerable with their stars aging and their thirst for championships quenched. Those fans could not have been more wrong.

Celtics 4
Lakers 0
Best Player: Bill Russell, Boston

CHAPTER 2

THE 1960s

1960
Boston Celtics vs. St. Louis Hawks

Coach Red Auerbach's Celtic squad did not change significantly from the previous year. Bill Russell still manned the middle with ferocious efficiency, Bob Cousy remained the league's premier point guard, and Bill Sharman and Tom Heinsohn ravaged opponents with their mid-range shooting. One lineup move was dictated when Jim Loscutoff went down with a back injury and Auerbach turned to Frank Ramsey, who thrived in his new starting role. Sam Jones, Gene Conley, and K.C. Jones were the biggest contributors off the bench. Boston upped its record in the regular season to 59-16 and then faced the much improved Philadelphia Warriors and their rookie center, Wilt Chamberlain, in the playoffs. He and Russell had staged some epic battles during the regular season, and these confrontations continued during the playoffs. Though Philly gave Boston all it could handle, the Celtics advanced to the finals, 4 games to 2.

The St. Louis Hawks—at the behest of their impatient owner, Bob Kerner—retooled for the 1959-60 campaign. Ed Macauley, now in his second year as coach,

guided a team that had plenty of firepower in the frontcourt. Joining stalwarts Bob Pettit and Cliff Hagan in the starting lineup was Clyde Lovellette, and all three averaged better than 20 points a night. When they tired, Larry Foust and Dave Piontek picked up the slack. The Hawks, however, were thin in the backcourt. Slater Martin was beginning to look his age at this point, and his partner, Johnny McCarthy, was unproven at the championship level. St. Louis relied on its excellent frontline scoring to go 46-29 and win the Western Division. In the playoffs, the Hawks survived a 7-game struggle with the Minneapolis Lakers, but suffered a tough blow when Martin was lost for the rest of the way to an injury.

With Si Green taking over at the point for St. Louis, the Celtics held a tremendous backcourt edge in the finals. That was evident in Game 1 at the Boston Garden, as Cousy helped engineer a 140-122 rout. But the hardnosed Hawks refused to go quietly, silencing the Boston faithful in Game 2 by a score of 113-103. Aggravated by the loss, Russell and crew dominated Game 3 at St. Louis's Kiel Auditorium. Keeping Pettit, Hagan, and Lovellette in check, the Celtics won 102-86. The Hawks then evened the series at 2-2 with a gritty 106-96 victory.

TEAM SPIRIT
THE 1960s: BOSTON CELTICS

During the 1960s, the Celtics went to the NBA Finals nine times and won nine championships. No team in professional sports has ever come close to matching this record. Add to this the championships won by Boston in 1957 and 1959, and the record is even more amazing.

Coach Red Auerbach had been around pro basketball for a long time and had developed a vision of what it would take to build a dynasty. He needed players who had star-level ability but who were willing to contribute that talent to a true team effort. In an era when scoring was on the rise, this was not an easy thing to ask players to do.

In his first few years as Celtic coach, Auerbach's teams did not reach the finals. This was a source of great frustration, for he had a trio of world-class guards in Bob Cousy, Bill Sharman, and Frank Ramsey, who bought into his system.

By the late 1950s, however, all the pieces were falling into place. Bill Russell, a mobile center who played great defense, triggered the Celtic offense with his ferocious rebounds and outlet passes. Tom Heinsohn, a sharpshooting forward, gave Auerbach instant offense on the front line. Boston won it all in 1957 and 1959, and began stockpiling talent on the bench to fuel its dynasty.

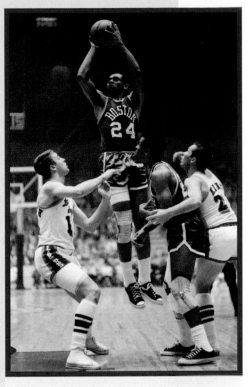

Sam Jones uses a teammate's screen to create an open jump shot. Jones was one of Boston's most prolific scorers during their championship years.

The players who sat and watched those early championships were the ones who stepped up when Sharman, Cousy, and Ramsey slowed down. Sam Jones, a big, quick guard with a sweet shot he liked to kiss off the backboard, became a starter and could be counted upon for 20 points a night. K.C. Jones, a defensive-minded backcourt player, shut down opposing scorers and ran the team after Cousy retired. Satch Sanders gave the club great defense and rebounding at one of the forward spots, and John Havlicek became the league's best sixth man. Russell remained the constant—the one Celtic who played on all eleven of the Boston championship teams in the '50s and '60s. When Auerbach retired, Russell both coached and starred at center for the 1969 championship team.

Boston's dominance finally came to an end after Russell's retirement in 1969, although by 1974 the Celtics had rebuilt and were champions again. Only NBA Hall of Famer John Havlicek remained as a link with Boston to their glory years of the 1960s.

In Boston for Game 5, the Celtics were in command from the opening tap, taking a lopsided 127-102 decision. Once again, however, St. Louis surged to victory on their home floor, which sent both teams to the Boston Garden for Game 7. This time, the Celtics didn't fool around. With Russell grabbing 35 rebounds, there were no second shots for the Hawks. Cousy contributed 19 points and 14 assists in a 122-103 rout that delivered a second straight title to Boston.

> Celtics 4
> Hawks 3
> Best Player: Bill Russell, Boston

1961
Boston Celtics vs. St. Louis Hawks

By the spring of 1961, the Celtics were poised to equal the old Lakers' record of three straight NBA titles. Red Auerbach's troops had raced to another Eastern Division crown with a record of 57-22. Their formula for winning was simple. Bill Russell patrolled the paint on defense, igniting the Celtics' fast break by blocking shots and cleaning the boards. Bob Cousy ran the fast break like a magician. The supporting cast of Tom Heinsohn, Frank Ramsey, Bill Sharman, Sam Jones, and K.C. Jones filled in with clutch scoring and solid defense. When the post-season rolled around, Boston was firing on all cylinders. The Celtics ran roughshod over the Syracuse Nationals in 5 games to reach the finals for the fifth year in a row.

This year's victim would be the St. Louis Hawks again. The team's volatile owner, Bob Kerner, had dismissed Ed Macauley and hired Paul Seymour. The new coach used the same starting five from the previous year's finals—Bob Pettit, Cliff Hagan, Clyde Lovellette, Si Green, and Johnny McCarthy— but rookie Lenny Wilkens was now the team's key contributor off the bench. St. Louis was never seriously challenged for the Western Division crown during the regular season, posting a record of 51-28. In the playoffs, the Hawks were tested by the Lakers, who were playing with renewed passion after moving from Minneapolis to Los Angeles, California. The grueling, seven-game series took its toll on St. Louis, which did not bode well for their chances against Boston.

The Celtics saw an opportunity to clip the Hawks' wings and seize an early advantage in the finals. In Game 1, they did just that with a 129-95 blowout. It was more of the same in Game 2, as Boston cruised again, this time by a score of 116-108. The Hawks gained a measure of revenge in Game 3, when they returned home to Kiel Auditorium and won 124-120. But Cousy and his teammates struck back in the next contest with a 119-104 laugher. At one point, Seymour became so frustrated that he seemed ready to throw a punch at the Boston point guard. Menacing forward Jim Loscutoff would have none of it, however, making it clear to the St. Louis coach that Cousy was not to be touched. Game 5 back at the Boston Garden was little more than a formality. Russell set the tone early when he blocked a shot, then beat everyone down the floor to finish the play with a layup. In his team's 121-112 win, he totaled 30 points and 38 rebounds, while Cousy added 18 points and 12 assists. But the championship was perhaps most meaningful to Sharman, who decided to retire despite being in phenomenal physical condition.

Celtics 4
Hawks 1
Best Player: Bill Russell, Boston

1962
Boston Celtics vs.
Los Angeles Lakers

The 1961-62 campaign was a season of change in the NBA. More teams were playing athletic, up-tempo basketball—and playing it above the rim. Many veterans of 1950s-style ball found themselves unable to cope with the big, agile players coming out of college.

The immediate result was an increase in the number of points the teams scored in a game. For Philadelphia, Wilt Chamberlain averaged 50.4 points a night for the Warriors and scored a record 100 points in a meeting with the New York Knicks.

One thing that didn't change was the dominance of the deep and experienced Celtics squad. Even against Chamberlain, they could do no wrong. Though Bob Cousy was starting to slow down, Bill Russell was at the apex of his powers. The same was true of his frontcourt mate, gunner Tom Heinsohn, who was nicknamed "Ack-Ack" after the rapid-firing anti-aircraft guns used by the military. Bankshot artist Sam Jones and defensive whiz Tom "Satch" Sanders joined the first string, giving the Celtics a pair of tough and intelligent new starters. When Boston needed a lift off the bench, Red Auerbach looked to old reliables Frank Ramsey and K.C. Jones.

In short, there was no situation the Celtics faced that could not be instantly addressed and ultimately overcome. Boston took its sixth-straight Eastern Division title with a

record of 60-20. In the playoffs, Chamberlain and the Warriors pushed Boston to Game 7, but the Celts won, 109-107.

Boston's opponent in the finals was the Lakers, a team on the rise. Los Angeles was a two-headed monster that terrorized defenses with the scoring of Elgin Baylor and the clutch shooting and suffocating defense of guard Jerry West. Both poured in better than 30 points a game, and either could take over a contest on any given night. Assembled around them was a collection of steady pros, including starters Rudy LaRusso, Jim Krebs, and Frank Selvy. Tom Hawkins and Hot Rod Hundley did most of the damage off the bench, though coach Fred Schaus re-

K.C. Jones gets a step on Jerry West of the Lakers. Jones was a master defender and incomparable floor leader for the great Celtic teams of the 1960s.

lied mostly on his first five. That strategy helped the Lakers to a 54-26 record and first-place finish in the West in the regular season. Los Angeles then battled the Detroit Pistons for the right to square off against the Celtics for the championship, winning that series in 6 games.

The finals opened in the Boston Garden, where the Celtics hoped to have their way with the happy-go-lucky Lakers. That is how it played out in Game 1, as Boston used a balanced attack to throttle Los Angeles, 122-108. But the next night, Baylor and West led a scoring barrage that produced a 129-122 Lakers win. When the series moved to Los Angeles for Game 3, a record crowd of 15,180 packed the Sports Arena. The Lakers put on a show with a dramatic 117-115 victory. As time wound down, West scored the go-ahead hoop on a lay-up after stealing an inbounds pass intended for Cousy. Impossible to rattle, the Celtics stormed back in Game 4 with a 115-103 win. In Boston for Game 5, the Celtics watched helplessly as Baylor burned them with 61 points—a new finals record—and 22 rebounds in a 126-121 victory by the Lakers.

Facing elimination, Boston went into the Sports Arena for Game 6 and controlled the action from the outset, cruising to a 119-105 triumph. This meant the championship would be decided on the Celtics' home floor. Game 7 opened with the Boston players appearing more relaxed, and they seized a 53-47 lead at intermission. But West and Baylor heated up, enabling the Lakers to pull even in the fourth quarter. With only minutes remaining, the Celtics went up by four points on clutch free throws by Russell and Sam Jones. An unlikely hero then sparked Los Angeles, as Selvy snuck into the lane for consecutive put-backs. With

time running out and the score knotted at 100-100, the veteran guard found himself open again. This time, however, Selvy's short jump shot rolled out, and the contest went to overtime. The Celtics knew they had dodged a bullet and turned it up a notch in the extra period. They won 110-107, for their fourth straight championship.

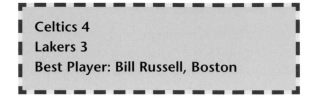

Celtics 4
Lakers 3
Best Player: Bill Russell, Boston

1963
Boston Celtics vs. Los Angeles Lakers

Haters of the Boston Celtics thought they finally had a glimmer of hope heading into the 1962-63 campaign. Before the season, Bob Cousy announced that this would be his last year. At 34, with 12 superlative seasons to his name, the man who did so much to change pro basketball now saw the game passing him by. That didn't mean he wasn't ready for one more run at a championship. Coach Red Auerbach's starting five—Bill Russell, Tom Heinsohn, Satch Sanders, Sam Jones, and Cousy—was the exact same as the year before, though the aging point guard spent more and more time watching from the bench. The Celtics, however, lost little when the less-dynamic K.C. Jones ran the offense. John Havlicek, a heady rookie out of Ohio State, also made big contributions off the bench, as did Frank Ramsey. Boston again took the Eastern Division handily with a record of 58-22, but encountered another stiff test in the playoffs, this time from Oscar Robertson and the Cincinnati Royals. As they had done so many times before, the Celtics came out on top, winning Game 7 on their home floor.

On the other coast, the Los Angeles Lakers were eager for another shot at Boston. The team had been fine-tuned in the off-season, adding stylish Dick Barnett to its backcourt and moving Frank Selvy to the bench. Still, the Lakers revolved around Elgin Baylor and Jerry West. The duo again enjoyed All-Star seasons, though West missed 25 games with a leg injury. But that didn't stop Los Angeles from taking the Western Division with a record of 53-27. In

Keith Erickson of the Lakers has no place to go, as Bill Russell prepares to swat his shot. Boston's great center dominated the middle for 11 Celtic champions.

the playoffs, coach Fred Schaus shuffled Gene Wiley and Jim Krebs in and out at center, while forward Rudy LaRusso did most of the dirty work down low. With West healthy, the Lakers still had their hands full with the resurgent St. Louis Hawks. On the strength of four victories in the Sports Arena, they won the series 4 games to 3 and advanced to the finals.

For the Celtics and their fans, the emotion of the finals was hard to ignore. Cousy was suiting up for his last hurrah with Boston, and everyone wanted him to go out a champion. The series started on a promising note for the Celtics when they took Games 1 and 2. In the first contest, Boston emerged with a hard-fought 117-114 victory, thanks to several key buckets down the stretch from sharpshooters Heinsohn and Sam Jones. The Celtics had an easier time of it the next night, surging to a 113-106 win. In Game 3 in Los Angeles, West and Baylor combined for 80 points, and the Lakers crushed Boston 119-99. The Celts got back on track in Game 4. Building a 17-point lead in the second half, they worked the clock in the fourth quarter and held on to win, 108-105.

With the series heading back East, Cousy hoped to end his career with a flourish at the Boston Garden. The Lakers didn't cooperate. With West and Baylor again having their way, Los Angeles cruised to a 126-119 win. Cousy, uncharacteristically off his game, fouled out with just 12 points. Though Boston held a 3-2 series edge, some thought the younger Lakers were in the driver's seat. Russell and Havlicek set the tone early in Game 6 with their defense and rebounding. Down by 14 points at intermission, Los Angeles staged a stirring comeback in the second half and cut the Boston lead to a single basket with less than three minutes left. But

Heinsohn stole a pass and converted a lay-up. From there, the Celtics knew what to do. On each offensive possession, they put the ball in Cousy's hands and let him control the action. As the horn sounded on Boston's 112-109 victory and the team's fifth title in a row, he tossed the ball high in the air, hugged Auerbach, and was mobbed by his teammates. Though Cousy wasn't on his beloved parquet floor, he ended his storied career surrounded by friendly faces.

> Celtics 4
> Lakers 2
> Best Player: Bill Russell, Boston

1964
Boston Celtics vs. San Francisco Warriors

Bob Cousy was gone, but the Boston Celtics were as good as ever. Without their magician at the point, the Celtics turned up the defensive intensity, knowing they could no longer count on outscoring opponents. That strategy was music to the ears of Bill Russell, who assumed an even greater leadership role on the team. K.C. Jones replaced Cousy in the starting lineup, while Tom Heinsohn, Satch Sanders, and Sam Jones all continued to perform at a high level. When coach Red Auerbach needed an offensive spark, he looked to John Havlicek, who led the team in scoring despite coming off the bench. The Celtics captured the top spot in the Eastern Division with 59 wins against 21 losses, though the Cincinnati Royals and their two superstars—Oscar Robertson and Jerry Lucas—stayed hot on their trail throughout the regular season. Come the

postseason, however, Boston rolled, dispatching the Royals in five games to advance to the finals.

The San Francisco Warriors—who had moved from Philadelphia the previous season—hoped to play the role of giant-killer this year. Wilt Chamberlain, at the peak of his powers, had altered his game to involve his teammates more, and the Warriors surpassed the Lakers as the best in the West. The "Big Dipper's" supporting cast included tough Tom Meschery and Wayne Hightower at forward and Gary Phillips and Guy Rodgers in the backcourt. A couple of defensive gems, Nate Thurmond and Al Attles, contributed mightily off the bench. They were good players made even better by Chamberlain's unselfish play. The Warriors finished with 48 wins but had to weather a storm in the playoffs against the St. Louis Hawks, who pushed them to seven games in the conference finals.

The NBA's dream of a Chamberlain-Russell final had come true. The two great centers had begun to capture the public's imagination, and during the early 1960s they won over many fans who had previously only watched college basketball. Chamberlain was the more dominant player physically, but Russell seemed to always come up with something that would make his team the winner. When the series opened at the Boston Garden, experts were shocked to see Russell allow Chamberlain to receive the ball in the low post. Russell's plan was to entice Chamberlain into trying his favorite shot, the fadeaway jumper. Although the Warrior center made a high percentage of these attempts, the shot took him away from the boards. If he missed, the Celtics controlled the rebound every time and were able to trigger their vaunted fast break. The

Celtics won Game 1 by a score of 108-96. Game 2 also went to Boston, 124-101.

The Warriors regrouped when the series moved to California, claiming an easy 115-91 victory in Game 3. Boston, however, responded with a supreme effort the next night. Ineffective for the first three contests, Heinsohn awoke midway through Game 4 and sparked the Celtics to a 98-95 win. Back at the Boston Garden, the Warriors tried to rally but found themselves down by 11 points in the fourth quarter. Although they fought back to within a basket, Russell was there to slam the door. With time winding down, he rebounded a teammate's missed shot and jammed home the follow-up. Boston went on to win 105-99 for its sixth title in as many years. The hero was Russell, who proved to be as strong as he was smart.

> Celtics 4
> Warriors 1
> Best Player: Bill Russell, Boston

1965
Boston Celtics vs. Los Angeles Lakers

The Boston Celtics were marked men. Teams around the NBA schemed to find ways to beat the defending champs. The Philadelphia 76ers, formerly the Syracuse Nationals, made the biggest push when they acquired Wilt Chamberlain in a trade with the San Francisco Warriors the day after the 1965 All-Star Game. The Celtics, meanwhile, were playing with heavy hearts. Before the season started, team owner and founder Walter Brown passed away. Nevertheless, Boston broke from the gate to win

its first 11 games and the Celts finished with a sparkling 62-18 record. The team's fast break had slowed down, but its defensive intensity had increased. As always, Bill Russell was the fulcrum of this hardworking unit. K.C. Jones and Satch Sanders followed his lead, while Sam Jones, John Havlicek, and Tom Heinsohn provided the bulk of the offense. In their much-anticipated playoff struggle with the 76ers, each team won on its home floor, setting up a thrilling Game 7 in Boston. With the Celtics up 110-109 and seconds left, Havlicek stole an inbounds pass to seal the victory.

The Los Angeles Lakers, glad to see Chamberlain out of their conference, returned to the finals with a deep and talented team. Jerry West and Elgin Baylor combined to average nearly 60 points a game and over 80 minutes a night. Guard Dick Barnett and forward Rudy LaRusso could fill it up, too. Gene Wiley, Darrall Imhoff, and Leroy Ellis handled enemy big men, while Jim King and rookies Walt Hazzard and Don Nelson contributed valuable minutes off the bench. Coach Fred Schaus guided his squad to a record of 49-31 and first place in the Western Division, giving Los Angeles fans hope that this might be their year. But in the playoff opener against the Baltimore Bullets, Baylor went down with a devastating knee injury. Though the Lakers gutted out a series win—thanks mostly to the brilliance of West—the idea of facing Boston without one of their two leaders was not very promising.

The Celtics figured all they had to do to beat Los Angeles in the finals was slow West down. The strategy worked to perfection in Game 1, as K.C. Jones held the Laker star to 26 points in a 142-110 rout. West found more open shots in Game 2 and hit most of them, scoring 45 points. But he got little help from his teammates, and Boston took a commanding 2-0 series lead with a 129-123 victory. Game 3, in Los Angeles, featured another stirring performance from West. This time, Ellis, filling in for Baylor, backed him up with 29 points, propelling the Lakers to a 126-105 victory. That was the last highlight of the finals for Los Angeles. In Game 4, Sam Jones exploded for 37 points, as Boston cruised to a 112-99 win.

When the series returned to the Boston Garden, the Lakers had the look of a team that wanted to go home. Up by five at the half, the Celtics overwhelmed Los Angeles in the final two quarters. To start the last period, they scored 20 points before the Lakers registered their first bucket. The final score was 129-96. Afterwards, an exhausted Auerbach made it official that the following season would be his last on the sideline. Without the late Walter Brown, the job of running the Celtics was too burdensome, and he decided to concentrate on the business side of the club after one more year as coach.

Celtics 4
Lakers 1
Best Player: Bill Russell, Boston

For Jerry West, the subject of this psychadelic Sports Illustrated cover, the 1960s must have seemed like a bad dream. Six times he led the Lakers to the NBA finals, and six times they were beaten by the Boston Celtics.

1966
Boston Celtics vs. Los Angeles Lakers

For the first time in a long time, the Boston Celtics were not the hands-down favorite to capture an NBA championship. That honor was bestowed upon on the improved Philadelphia 76ers, who had assembled a strong supporting cast around Wilt Chamberlain. The role of underdog seemed to suit the Celtics. Red Auerbach, in his last season at the helm, realized his team was growing old. Tom Heinsohn had called it quits before the campaign began, and Bill Russell, Sam Jones, and K.C. Jones were all in their 30s. To combat the effects of age, Auerbach inserted John Havlicek into the starting lineup next to Satch Sanders at forward and plucked feisty Don Nelson off the waiver wire. Boston went 54-26 in the regular season and finished a game behind Philadelphia in the standings. The Celtics prevailed in an exhausting best-of-five playoff series against the Cincinnati Royals, then faced Philly for the right to move on to the finals. The Celtics found their second wind on Philly's home court, taking the opener. The 76ers never recovered, dropping three of the next four.

The Los Angeles Lakers also reached the championship round after an uphill struggle. With Elgin Baylor attempting a comeback from his knee injury, the team often seemed to be in disarray. Jerry West put the Lakers on his back and led them to a first-place finish in the Western Division with a record of 45-35. He got help from backcourt mate Walt Hazzard, who stepped into a starting role. Rudy LaRusso had another solid year opposite Baylor on the front line, while Leroy Ellis, Bob Boozer, and Darrall Imhoff all saw time at center. By the post-season, Baylor began flashing his old form, bolstering the confidence of coach Fred Schaus. The Lakers slugged it out with the St. Louis Hawks in the playoffs, earning another shot at the title after seven hard fought games.

Los Angeles could not have been more encouraged by what they saw in Game 1 of the finals. Down by 18 at Boston Garden, the Lakers battled back for a 133-129 overtime win. West and Baylor were magnificent, combining for 77 points. Afterwards, Auerbach made headlines when he revealed that Russell would take over next year as the team's coach. The announcement seemed to refocus the Celtics, who rolled to a 129-109 victory in Game 2. As the series shifted to Los Angeles, Boston sensed that Havlicek was posing serious match-up problems for the Lakers and Auerbach planned to go to him more and more. Schaus assigned LaRusso to guard the hard-working forward in Games 3 and 4, but he wasn't quick enough. Pressing this advantage, the Celtics went to Havlicek every time they needed a

bucket and won both contests at the Sports Arena, 120-106 and 122-117.

Back in Boston for Game 5, Schaus tried a new strategy, turning to speedy rookie Gail Goodrich and using LaRusso off the bench. The move worked, as the Lakers controlled Havlicek and pulled out a 121-117 victory. The trio of West, Baylor, and Goodrich did it again in Game 6, posting a 123-115 win in Los Angeles. Game 7 in Boston was a wild scene. The Celtics moved ahead early, but the Lakers charged back behind West and Baylor. With four seconds left, the Celtics were up 95-93 and about to inbound the ball. Boston's delirious fans couldn't wait for the last few ticks on the clock, however, and rushed on the court. In the confusion, K.C. Jones managed to pass to Havlicek, who dribbled until the horn sounded. For the ninth and last time as the Celtics' coach, Auerbach celebrated another championship by lighting one of his famous victory cigars.

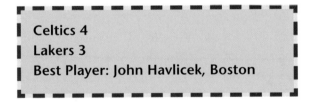

Celtics 4
Lakers 3
Best Player: John Havlicek, Boston

1967
Philadelphia 76ers vs. San Francisco Warriors

After playing second-fiddle to the aging Celtics for two seasons, the Philadelphia 76ers finally built a superb supporting cast around the great Wilt Chamberlain. Chet Walker, Billy Cunningham, and Luke Jackson filled out a versatile front line, while the backcourt tandem of Hal Greer and Wali Jones triggered an unstoppable offense. The real difference-maker, however, was coach Alex Hannum. Coaching Chamberlain for the second time, Hannum convinced his center to let his fellow players feed off of him, and to save his strength for defense and rebounding. For the first time since he joined the NBA, Chamberlain did not win the scoring title—and the 76ers won a record 68 games. The 76ers handled the Cincinnati Royals in the first round of the newly expanded playoffs, then over-whelmed the Celtics, now coached by Rus-sell, to advance to the finals.

The Warriors also built their team around a do-it-all superstar, 22-year-old Rick Barry. The 6'7" forward could shoot from anywhere on the floor and possessed ballhandling and passing skills that made him almost impossible to guard. San Fran-cisco had good size up front with Nate Thur-mond and Fred Hetzel, while Jeff Mullins and Paul Neumann were solid at guard. Tom Meschery, Al Attles, and Jim King—all ex-perienced bench players—were employed to perfection by ex-Celtic Bill Sharman, who had developed into a terrific coach after his playing days. In the post-season, the War-riors snuck past the Lakers then outplayed the Hawks to reach the finals.

The heavily favored 76ers, playing on their home floor in Convention Hall, got a scare in Game 1 of the finals when they al-most blew a 19-point lead. Barry hit for 37 and the Warriors pushed the contest into overtime, but Philadelphia regained its composure and won, 141-135. The next night, the 76ers left nothing to chance, con-trolling the pace for 48 minutes. Greer poured in 30 and Cunningham added 28 in a 126-95 blowout. When the series moved to San Francisco's Cow Palace, fans sensed the Warriors were on the verge of being

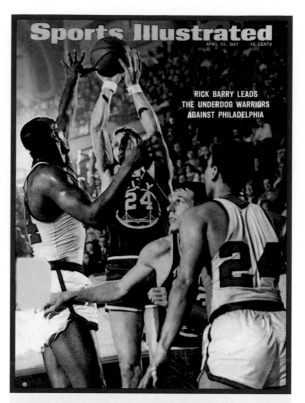

This Sports Illustrated cover captures Rick Barry shooting in traffic against the Philadelphia 76ers. The second-year scoring sensation made front-page news when he led the underdog Warriors to the NBA finals.

swept. Barry allayed those fears, piling up 55 points in a narrow 130-124 victory. Philadelphia got back to business in Game 4, as Greer and Walker combined for 71 points on the way to a 122-108 victory rout.

Up 3-1 in the series, the 76ers looked un-beatable—except to the Warriors. In Game 5, Barry exploded for 26 in the first half and his teammates finished off the surprised 76ers, 117-109. The loss had some fans whispering of a Philadelphia choke. When the Warriors matched the 76ers bucket for bucket early in Game 6, those whispers grew louder. Then, with Philly down by four in the fourth quarter, Hannum inserted rookie guard Matt Guokas, who canned two quick baskets. The momentum had swung, and the 76ers took the contest 125-122. Chamberlain's play against his old team proved the difference, as he neutralized San Francisco's inside game and let the other Philadelphia shooters take care of the scoring.

76ers 4
Warriors 2
Best Player: Wilt Chamberlain, Philadelphia

1968
Boston Celtics vs.
Los Angeles Lakers

The taunts of Philadelphia fans rang in the ears of the Boston Celtics all summer long in 1967. In the waning minutes of their playoff loss to the 76ers, Bill Russell and his players had to listen to Philly fans tell them they were through, that the Celtic era in the NBA was over. The Celts were determined to make them eat their words. With player-coach Russell at center, John Havlicek and Sam Jones in the backcourt, and Satch Sanders at forward, Boston's championship nucleus remained. New to the mix was veteran forward Bailey Howell. Larry Siegfried and Don Nelson were valuable contributors in reserve roles, giving Celtic fans hope that their beloved team had just enough depth to make one last run. A 54-28 record left Boston eight games behind the 76ers in the standings, but the Celtics survived a tough series against Dave Bing and the Pistons and then beat Philadelphia in seven games—winning the finale 100-96 on the enemy's home court.

The Los Angeles Lakers offered the Celtics a familiar foe in the finals. Their coach, Butch Van Breda Kolff, struggled through much of the year without Jerry West, who was hurt. Los Angeles acquired big man Erwin Mueller and guard Freddie Crawford in separate deals, and this duo provided needed depth to an otherwise thin club. Elgin Baylor carried as much of the load as his aching legs would allow, with help from guards Gail Goodrich and Archie Clark. Darrall Imhoff, Tom Hawkins, and Mel Counts kept opponents honest in the paint. When West returned to the lineup, the Lakers were almost unbeatable, and they demolished the Chicago Bulls and San Francisco Warriors in the playoffs to get yet another crack at the Celtics.

Though some of the faces had changed, the finals had all the elements of a classic Celtic-Laker war. Boston employed a swarming defense in Game 1 to corral West and Baylor and it paid off with a 107-101 win. The Lakers came back in Game 2, dealing Boston a 123-113 loss. From there, the series moved to the Great Western Forum, Los Angeles's luxurious new arena. The Celtics were up for the challenge and scored a 127-119 victory. The Lakers knotted the series the following night by a score of 119-105, their passions inspired by Van Breda Kolff's ejection in the second half. The win came at a high price. In the closing minutes, West sprained an ankle, and his status for the rest of the series was put in question.

Amazingly, the All-Star guard recovered in time to play in Game 5 at the Boston Garden, ringing up 35 points and forcing the contest into overtime. Russell made the key play in the extra period, rejecting a shot by Baylor, and the Celtics escaped with a 120-117 victory. In Game 6, at the Forum,

Russell showed that he learned a thing or two from Red Auerbach. He moved Sam Jones to forward, which created a match-up problem for the Lakers, and rode the hot hands of Havlicek and Howell to build a big lead. Boston cruised to a 124-109 win for its 10th NBA title in 12 seasons.

Celtics 4
Lakers 2
Best Player: John Havlicek, Boston

1969
Boston Celtics vs. Los Angeles Lakers

Boston made no significant additions to its roster in the off-season after winning it all in 1968. Bill Russell, realizing his team was getting old, made Sam Jones his sixth man and promoted reserve guard Larry Siegfried to the starting lineup. John Havlicek again led the team in scoring, Bailey Howell and Satch Sanders were as steady as ever up front, and Don Nelson and Em Bryant offered quality minutes off the bench. The rest of the Eastern Division had caught up to Boston, however, and the Celtics finished fourth at 48-34. In the playoffs, where experience is so important, Russell and his mates came alive, defeating the 76ers in five games and then stealing a series away from the fast-improving New York Knicks to make the finals.

Across the country, the Los Angeles Lakers appeared to finally have the right stuff. Over the summer, the team sent shockwaves throughout the league when it traded three players to Philadelphia to obtain Wilt Chamberlain. With Wilt the Stilt at center, Elgin Baylor at forward, and Jerry

West at guard, coach Butch van Breda Kolff had the most potent trio of superstars in NBA history. Joining these three in the starting lineup were forward Mel Counts and guard Johnny Egan. Off the bench, Keith Erickson, Tom Hawkins, Bill Hewitt, and Freddie Crawford provided youthful energy and veteran savvy. To no one's surprise, the Lakers marched to the best record in the Western Division at 55-27. In the playoffs, they handled a challenge from the San Francisco Warriors, then grounded the Atlanta Hawks, to reach the finals.

The Lakers felt a psychological edge heading into the series, thanks to a 108-73 dismantling of the Celtics in the last week of the regular season. Game 1 at the Forum, however, was hardly a blowout. Los Ange-

When Wilt Chamberlain joined Jerry West and Elgin Baylor on the Lakers, it was a national cover story.

les needed every one of West's 53 points and 10 assists to outlast Boston, 120-118. In Game 2, Havlicek tried to turn the tide, torching the Lakers for 43. But West was hot again and sparked his team to a 118-112 victory. When the series shifted to the Boston Garden, the Celtics were lifted by their raucous fans. In Game 3, Havlicek starred again, even after getting poked in the face by Erickson. With his left eye swollen shut, he hit all his free throws down the stretch in Boston's 111-105 win. Game 4 presented the Lakers with a chance to take command of the series. In an ugly contest that featured an excessive number of fouls and turnovers, Los Angeles led by 1 point with 15 seconds left. But Bryant, a starter for the Celtics only in the playoffs, stole the ball. After a timeout, Jones found himself open for an instant from 18 feet. His off-balance jumper barely cleared Chamberlain's outstretched hand, rattled around the rim, and then dropped in for an 89-88 victory that deadlocked the series.

The teams split the next two, with the Lakers taking Game 5 in Los Angles 117-104 and Boston winning at home, 99-90. Game 7 at the Forum opened with Havlicek and the Celtics on fire, but, by intermission, the Lakers had closed the gap. Russell, searching for a way to keep his exhausted teammates focused, pointed to the ceiling, where a net holding hundreds of balloons hovered high above the hardwood, waiting for the Lakers' victory celebration. The thought of those balloons falling provided the incentive the Celtics needed. In the second half, Boston went on a roll, building a 17-point lead early in the fourth quarter. West, hobbled by a sore hamstring, then rallied his teammates. The comeback suffered a setback, however, when Chamberlain landed awkwardly after a rebound and left the game. After his replacement, Counts, hit a jumper that cut the deficit to 103-102, Wilt declared himself ready to return, but Van Breda Kolff inexplicably kept him on the bench. Minutes later, Nelson hit a tough shot for Boston that put the contest out of reach. Afterwards, Russell and Havlicek visited the Los Angeles locker room to congratulate West, who was the best player in the game but had no championships to show for it. The All-Star guard was awarded the NBA's inaugural Finals MVP trophy—the first and last time a player from a losing team has been so honored.

Celtics 4
Lakers 3
Best Player: Jerry West, Los Angeles

CHAPTER 3

THE 1970s

1970
New York Knicks vs. Los Angeles Lakers

For a city that loved basketball as much as New York, the Big Apple had experienced little success in pro hoops. The Knicks had enjoyed a nice run in the early 1950s, advancing to the finals in three consecutive seasons, but never once took the championship. The 1969-70 Knicks were eager to write a new chapter in the city's basketball history. Under the guidance of coach Red Holzman, the team rounded into form, playing balanced and disciplined team ball. Center Willis Reed was the squad's leading scorer and rebounder. Flanking him were a pair of hard-working forwards, Bill Bradley and Dave DeBusschere. In the backcourt, veteran Dick Barnett steadied the flamboyant Walt Frazier, an emerging star who starred at both ends of the floor. Mike Riordan, Cazzie Russell, and Dave Stallworth gave Holzman three reliable contributors off the bench. New York surged to the top of the Eastern Division with a record of 60-22. After disposing of the Baltimore Bullets in a tense seven-game series, the Knicks vanquished rookie Lew Alcindor and the Milwaukee Bucks to move on to the finals.

Still smarting from their heartbreaking loss the year before, the Los Angeles Lakers started the 1969-70 campaign as if suffering from a hangover. Wilt Chamberlain and Elgin Baylor both spent long periods on the sidelines with knee injuries, putting the pressure on Jerry West to carry the team. He did of course, with help from support players like Happy Hairston, Dick Garrett, Mel Counts, Rick Roberson, Keith Erickson, and Willie McCarter. When Chamberlain and Baylor finally returned, coach Joe Mullaney had a team that no one wanted to face in the playoffs. After finishing second in the Western Division at 46-36, Los Angeles edged the Phoenix Suns, winning Game 7 at the Forum. Now on a roll, the Lakers swept their next series against the Hawks to advance.

Madison Square Garden was electric before Game 1. Early on, the Knicks used the crowd's energy to sprint ahead by 20 points, but the experienced Lakers fought back to take a three-point lead in the fourth quarter. Then New York turned up the defensive intensity and raced to a 124-112 win. After being outplayed by Reed, Chamberlain came into Game 2 determined to turn the tables. The Los Angeles center was everywhere on defense, including a key

Knick trainer Danny Whelan escorts injured Willis Reed to the locker room during Game 5 of the 1970 finals. Reed's return for Game 7 sparked New York to a dramatic win.

Back in New York for Game 5, the Knicks were nearly perfect on defense, forcing 30 turnovers in a decisive 107-100 victory. But along the way they lost Reed to a torn thigh muscle. His absence was felt in Game 6 in Los Angeles, as Chamberlain racked up 45 points and 27 rebounds in a 135-113 blowout. Prior to Game 7, the sellout crowd at Madison Square Garden had resigned itself to another ugly defeat when, somehow, Reed limped out of the locker room at the end of warm-ups. He was greeted with a deafening roar, and even the Lakers stopped to admire Reed's courage. When the game began, the Knicks captain hit two jumpers over Chamberlain and the Garden went wild. Frazier played the game of his career, with 36 points, 19 assists, and a dozen great defensive plays, as the Knicks rolled to a 113-99 win. Though Reed tallied just four points and three rebounds in Game 7, he was awarded the MVP trophy at the end of the game.

> Knicks 4
> Lakers 3
> Best Player: Willis Reed, New York

block in the waning seconds to secure a 105-103 victory by the Lakers. Game 3 at the Forum found the Lakers down by two points with three seconds remaining. Chamberlain inbounded the ball to West, who dribbled three times and then heaved the ball toward the Knicks basket from 55 feet away. The shot hit nothing but net, forcing an overtime. The Knicks hung tough, however, and won 111-108. Game 4 was just as tense, but this time it went to Los Angeles in overtime by a score of 121-115.

1971
Baltimore Bullets vs. Milwaukee Bucks

Normally, it takes an expansion team several years before it can compete at a championship level. But Lew Alcindor was not your normal center, and he made the Bucks more than the normal expansion team. After leading UCLA to three national titles, the agile 7'2" big man joined the Milwaukee Bucks in 1969. The club became an instant

TWO-MAN GAME

KAREEM ABDUL-JABBAR AND OSCAR ROBERTSON

After just one NBA season, the expansion Milwaukee Bucks landed the best player in the history of college basketball, Lew Alcindor. The seven-footer, who later changed his name to Kareem Abdul-Jabbar, was as good in the pros as he had been at UCLA. Even with a lackluster supporting cast, the team won 56 games in his rookie year. But that spring, during the 1970 playoffs, the Bucks were routed by the mature and experienced New York Knicks.

When superstar guard Oscar Robertson became available over the winter, Milwaukee leapt at the chance to get him. The "Big O" was the perfect man to run a team with the game's best young big man. Robertson had spent a decade with the Cincinnati Royals, and averaged a triple-double every night during those years. He could do it all, but could the veteran accept doing less so that his towering teammate could lead the Bucks to the finals?

Not a problem. Robertson controlled the tempo on offense, shut down opposing guards on defense, and took 500 fewer shots than he had in his glory years. When Abdul-Jabbar was double-teamed, Robertson would calmly find the open man with a pinpoint pass or back his man toward the basket and swish his patented turnaround jumper. Few remembered that he had experience at two-man basketball. When Robertson first came into the league, he teamed with forward Jack Twyman, and later with Jerry Lucas, to ravage enemy defenses. Meshing with the big, young center was like riding a bicycle.

In 1970-71, the Bucks were literally unbeatable at times, putting together winning streaks of 16 and 20 games. They finished the year with 66 wins despite playing in the NBA's toughest division, then dropped just two games in the playoffs on their way to the championship.

contender, but it still lacked a veteran star to guide its fortunes. Enter Oscar Robertson, the 31-year-old guard who had done everything a player could do in 10 seasons with the Cincinnati Royals but reach the NBA finals. The "Big O" provided the missing ingredient in a lineup that included forwards Greg Smith and Bob Dandridge and guard Jon McGlocklin. Bob Boozer and Lucius Allen were quality bench players for coach Larry Costello who guided Milwaukee to a 66-16 finish. In the playoffs, the Bucks obliterated the San Francisco Warriors and Los Angeles Lakers to advance to their first finals.

The Baltimore Bullets had the unenviable task of trying to stop the streaking Bucks. Coached by Gene Shue, the Bullets had an intriguing mix of players. Earl "The Pearl" Monroe was the league's flashiest

Oscar Robertson tries a fadeaway against the Lakers in the 1971 playoffs. The "Big O" brought his trademark one-handed jumper and peerless leadership to Milwaukee and won a championship.

42-40. Then the Bullets registered two seven-game upsets in the postseason, first beating the Philadelphia 76ers and then derailing the New York Knicks.

Baltimore's grueling playoff run took its toll. Monroe, Unseld, and Johnson were all ailing, their status uncertain from game to game. That was bad news for the Bullets, because Milwaukee was fully rested. The Bucks won Game 1 on their home floor in impressive fashion 98-88. Though he got into early foul trouble, Alcindor finished with 31 points, doing most of his damage in the second half. The series shifted to Baltimore for Game 2, but the result was pretty much the same. In a 102-83 victory, the experienced and highly physical Robertson shackled Monroe, holding him to 11 points while scoring with 22 himself. Back in Milwaukee for Game 3, the Bucks continued to look sharp, winning 107-99. This time Dandridge topped the scoring list with 29 points. The series ended two nights later in Baltimore. With Robertson hitting for 30, Milwaukee cruised, 118-106, to notch the only second sweep in finals history.

> Bucks 4
> Bullets 0
> MVP: Lew Alcindor, Milwaukee

1972
New York Knicks vs. Los Angeles Lakers

So many times in his long career, Jerry West had come close to an NBA championship, only to have it torn from his grasp. That was to change in the spring of 1972. West's Los Angeles Lakers entered the regular season

guard, while center Wes Unseld was as tough to move as a tree stump. Unseld was flanked by hard-working Jack Marin and high-flying Gus Johnson. Monroe's mate in the backcourt was Kevin Loughery, whose intensity kept the team focused. Fred Carter, Eddie Miles, and John Tresvant got most of the minutes off the bench. Baltimore benefited from playing in the moribund Central Division, taking first place with a record of as one of many teams with a chance at a title. With taskmaster Bill Sharman taking over as coach, the squad possessed the focus and discipline it had lacked in the past. The triumvirate of West, Wilt Chamberlain, and Elgin Baylor lasted just nine games before Baylor's knee gave out, but in stepped 23-year-old Jim McMillian, who energized the club with his outside shooting. Other additions to the starting lineup were forward Happy Hairston and guard Gail Goodrich,

Wilt Chamberlain strains to get a hand on Kareem Abdul-Jabbar's famous sky hook. The two superstars faced off in the 1972 playoffs, with Chamberlain advancing to play the Knicks in the finals.

who blossomed into the Lakers' top scorer. Off the bench, Pat Riley, Leroy Ellis, and Flynn Robinson hustled and played strong defense. Los Angeles went from November 5 to January 7 without a loss, winning a record 33 games in a row. The club's final mark of 69-13 was the best in NBA history. In the playoffs, the Lakers manhandled the Chicago Bulls and then defeated the cocksure Milwaukee Bucks in six games.

After a so-so regular season, the New York Knicks hit their stride in the playoffs. The team looked a bit different from its championship year of 1970, thanks to injuries and acquisitions. Willis Reed went down with a bad knee and was replaced at center by Jerry Lucas, picked up in a trade with the San Francisco Warriors. Lucas owned an odd-looking long-range jumper that drew opposing big men out to the perimeter. This opened up all sorts of possibilities for Walt Frazier and Earl Monroe, whom the Knicks acquired for a couple of players and a lot of cash. Dave DeBusschere and Bill Bradley were joined on the forward line by Phil Jackson, who provided staunch defense off the bench. It took almost a full season for this group to meld, but once it did, New York was hard to stop. The Knicks buried the Bullets and Celtics in the playoffs and prepared to do battle with Wilt and West.

Based on Game 1 at the Forum in Los Angeles, it appeared the Lakers were in deep trouble. In a surprisingly easy 114-92 victory, the Knicks shot brilliantly, with Bradley and Lucas doing the most damage. But bad luck struck New York in Game 2 when DeBusschere was injured in the first half. That opened the floor for Hairston, who led Los Angeles to a 106-92 win. As the series shifted to Madison Square Garden for Game 3, DeBusschere decided he would

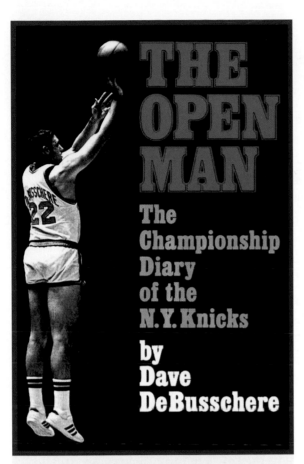

The title of Dave DeBusschere's chronicle of the 1969-70 championship season says it all about the Knicks' philosophy: Find the open man. Passing and teamwork transformed a collection of good players into a great club.

try to play, but he was clearly at less than 100 percent. The Lakers, in turn, sprinted to a 22-point lead and coasted to 107-96.

In Game 4, the injury bug bit Chamberlain when he fell in the first quarter and sprained a wrist. But the big man refused to go to the bench, and he helped Los Angeles push the contest into overtime. In the extra period, Chamberlain picked up his intensity on defense, even though he had five fouls.

Wilt had never fouled out of a game in his career, but he happily risked a sixth whistle with a chance to seize control of the series. His inspired performance spelled the difference in a 116-111 win. The question before Game 5 back in Los Angeles was whether Chamberlain's wrist injury would keep him from suiting up. But not only did the big man answer the bell, he controlled the contest from start to finish. Posting 24 points and 29 rebounds, Chamberlain laid claim to the series MVP as the Lakers rolled to the title 114-100. Afterwards, West was both exuberant and relieved. At long last the owner of an NBA championship, he raised a glass and toasted Chamberlain.

Lakers 4
Knicks 1
MVP: Wilt Chamberlain, Los Angeles

1973
New York Knicks vs. Los Angeles Lakers

The New York Knicks' starting five was perhaps the most talented in the league during the 1972-73 season. Willis Reed was back at center, although injuries left him less dominant than in the past. Bill Bradley and Dave DeBusschere were intelligent forwards who provided clutch scoring. In the backcourt, Walt Frazier and Earl Monroe had learned to share the ball, making them the most dangerous duo in the NBA. Guard Dean Meminger and forwards Jerry Lucas and Phil Jackson gave coach Red Holzman just enough off the bench. The Knicks compiled a 57-25 record, finishing second to the fast-improving Boston Celtics. In the play-

TEAM SPIRIT
THE 1970s: NEW YORK KNICKS

No team during the 1970s won two championships in a row, so it is impossible to pick "the" team of the decade. Although the retooled Los Angeles Lakers—with Wilt Chamberlain, Jerry West, and Gail Goodrich—put together some amazing seasons, it was the New York Knicks who pioneered a new kind of team basketball that provided the championship formula for many years.

At a time when the NBA was becoming bigger, faster, and more athletic, the Knicks lacked a superstar player who could take the team and carry it on his back. In fact, at first glance, New York was far from imposing. Center Willis Reed was a converted 6'10" power forward, while power forward Dave DeBusschere was only an inch or two taller than most backcourt players. Bill Bradley was a slow-footed small forward, Cazzie Russell could score but was an unenthusiastic defender, and Dick Barnett was a stylish but aging guard. Walt Frazier, the team's best player, was smart and opportunistic, a combination of defensive strength and offensive creativity. Later additions, including superstars Jerry Lucas and Earl Monroe, learned how to work their games into the Knicks' team concept and became valuable contributors.

Coach Red Holzman devised a system that accentuated his players' talents and masked their flaws. He had them play a complex, switching defense that was almost like a zone. It kept mismatches to a minimum and saved the players' strength. Holzman stressed fundamentals, like boxing out on rebounds and contesting every shot. On offense, the Knicks were disciplined passers, patiently working the ball around until they found an open man. Teams would lose to the Knicks and not understand how. As Holzman's players gained confidence, they got even better. When they needed a big game from someone, they usually got it—although you never knew who that player might be.

In 1970, and again in 1973, the Knicks proved that a well-coached, close-knit team could defeat more talented opponents and win a championship by staying focused and executing well. Though injuries and age prevented the Knicks from winning more NBA titles, during their heyday they were the league's most respected club.

offs, the Knicks trounced the Baltimore Bullets, then beat the Celtics in a fierce seven-game series.

Meanwhile, Jerry West, Wilt Chamberlain, Gail Goodrich, Happy Hairston, and Jim McMillian were anxious to defend their title. When Hairston hurt his knee, coach Bill Sharman turned to old-timer Bill Bridges, who was backed up by Keith Erickson and Mel Counts. This veteran crew captured the top spot in the Pacific Division with a record of 60-22. Their first postseason match-up came against the stingy Chicago Bulls, who pushed them to Game 7 before falling 95-92. After that wake-up call, the Lakers breezed by the Golden State Warriors in five games to move on to the finals.

The Knicks, a tired bunch, arrived in Los Angeles for Game 1. Their series against Boston had drained them and it showed, as the Lakers jumped to a 20-point lead on their way to a 115-112 victory. Chamberlain was a monster, blocking seven shots and altering countless others. New York rallied back in Game 2, stopping the Los Angeles fast break with a terrific defensive effort. They were spurred on by an unlikely hero on offense, as Jackson netted 17 points. When the series moved to Madison Square Garden for Game 3, Reed made his presence felt. With DeBusschere and Bradley struggling from the field, the New York center knocked down one big jumper after another. Monroe then heated up in the fourth quarter, and the Knicks won 87-83.

Game 4 went right down to the wire. With less than a minute left, DeBusschere picked up a loose ball after Reed kept a rebound alive against the towering Chamberlain. When he sank the put-back and was fouled, New York got the buffer it needed and triumphed by a score of 103-98. In Game 5, both teams seemed a bit tight. The contest stayed close until the final period, when Monroe exploded for 8 points over a two-minute stretch. The scoring spree salted away a 102-93 victory and gave New York its second championship.

> **Knicks 4**
> **Lakers 1**
> **MVP: Willis Reed, New York**

1974
Boston Celtics vs. Milwaukee Bucks

For five years, the Boston Celtics had been denied post-season glory. With ties to the dynasty of the 1950s and 1960s fading, the team hoped to embark on a new era of greatness. There were still reminders of their proud past. Tom Heinsohn was now on the sidelines as Boston's coach, John Havlicek, was the team's top scorer, and Don Nelson remained a valuable bench player. The rest of the cast, however, had changed. Dave Cowens, an undersized center with the heart of a giant, was a fiery leader on and off the court. Forward Paul Silas, a rock-solid rebounder and defender, joined a starting five that also included guards Don Chaney and Jo Jo White. Heinsohn was so confident in his starters that he almost never used his bench, especially at crunch time. After taking the Atlantic Division with a 56-26 mark, Boston faced a stiff challenge from Bob McAdoo and the upstart Buffalo Braves in the first round of playoffs. The Celtics weathered that storm and then blitzed the aging New York Knicks to reach the finals.

Their opponent was the team that everyone had expected to embark on a long run of championships two years earlier: the Milwaukee Bucks. The team had made several questionable personnel moves, however, that robbed the club of its chemistry. Still, with Kareem Abdul-Jabbar (formerly Lew Alcindor) in the middle, the Bucks were a scary squad. Bob Dandridge remained from the title team at one forward, while Curtis Perry now flanked him at the other spot. In the backcourt, Lucius Allen slid into the lineup next to Oscar Robertson, who was slowing down significantly at age

36. Unfortunately for the Bucks, injuries ravaged them heading into the playoffs. Allen hurt his knee, forcing subs Jon Mc-Glocklin and Ron Williams to start in his place. Coach Larry Costello also worked forward Cornell Warner into the mix. But Abdul-Jabbar was magnificent in the post-season, carrying the Bucks over the Los Angeles Lakers in five games and then over the Chicago Bulls in four.

The finals opened in Milwaukee, and the Celtics immediately attacked the Bucks' weaknesses. Exploiting the uneven ballhandling skills of Robertson, McGlocklin, and Williams, they forced one turnover after another en route to a 98-83 victory in Game 1. The next night, Abdul-Jabbar took control, scoring 36 points and setting up teammates on many other occasions for easy shots. The result was a 105-96 win by the Bucks. In Game 3 in the Boston Garden, Cowens moved outside and relied on his jump shot to score 30 points. With Boston again playing harassing defense, the Celtics cruised 95-83. Coach Costello gambled in Game 4, inserting a flashy reserve named Mickey Davis into the lineup. The switch clearly confused the Celtics, who couldn't stop the Bucks in the low post and lost 97-89.

When the series shifted back to Milwaukee, Havlicek emerged as a hero for Boston. In constant motion, the 33-year-old ran Buck defenders ragged, and the Celtics won 96-87. Game 6 had fans in Boston anticipating another title. But Abdul-Jabbar showed why he was regarded as the NBA's best player. Down the stretch in regulation, he turned it on at both ends of the court. With time running down in overtime and Milwaukee trailing by a point, he swished a 17-foot hook shot for a dramatic 102-101 victory. In Game 7, Havlicek was again

John Havlicek looks for the open man. His unselfish play made him a valuable sixth man and, later, one of the NBA's greatest superstars.

magnificent. With the Bucks bound and determined to stop him, Cowens was able to shake free from Abdul-Jabbar time and again. The redheaded center made them pay with 28 points and 14 rebounds. Though Havlicek scored only 16, he was the key as the Celtics won 102-87. Their 12th championship was their first without Bill Russell.

Celtics 4
Bucks 3
MVP: John Havlicek, Boston

1975
Baltimore Bullets vs. Golden State Warriors

Prior to the 1974-75 season, the NBA waved goodbye to some of its greatest stars. Jerry West, Willis Reed, and Oscar Robertson all retired, and Wilt Chamberlain defected to the ABA. After the campaign ended, the league said hello to a new champion. The Golden State Warriors (formerly San Francisco) had been knocking on the door in the Pacific Division for years. Led by do-it-all veteran Rick Barry, the team finally broke through in the spring of 1975. Coach Al Attles put up with Barry's brashness and focused the offensive gameplan around his talented forward. The rest of the squad thought defense first. Young forward Keith Wilkes played D like a veteran and could score, too. At center, Cliff Ray flexed his muscles on the boards, and George Johnson—a gangly shot-blocker—provided quality minutes as his substitute. Guards Butch Beard and Charlie Johnson both averaged in double figures, but their main responsibility was disrupting a foe's offensive rhythm. And backcourt reserve Phil Smith was always ready with some instant offense. Golden State won its division with a record of 48-34 and then took two hard-fought victories in the playoffs, first beating the Seattle Supersonics in six games and then outlasting the Chicago Bulls in seven. The Warriors were not a particularly good team on paper, but each man knew his role, and everyone always looked to help their teammates.

By contrast, the Washington Bullets (formerly from Baltimore) were a powerhouse. Their best player was forward Elvin Hayes, a scoring machine who was unstoppable when he was on. Guard Phil Chenier could fill it up as well, while his backcourt partner, Kevin Porter, was an unparalleled assist man. Wes Unseld still patrolled the middle at center, able to ignite a potent fast break with strong rebounding and perfect outlet passes. Forward Mike Riordan was a dependable scorer and defender, while Nick Weatherspoon provided muscle off the bench. With former Celtic K.C. Jones as coach, the team also had a proven leader who knew all about postseason pressure. The Bullets sped away from the competition in the Central Division with a record of 60-22. In the playoffs, after Jones moved Weatherspoon into the starting lineup for Riordan, they squeaked by the Buffalo Braves in seven games before overcoming the Boston Celtics in six.

Experts gave Golden State little chance, if any, in the finals, and Washington confidently agreed. In fact, because of a scheduling error at the Oakland Coliseum Arena, the Bullets agreed to play Game 1 at home, the next two on the road, and then return to the capital region for Game 4. This decision seemed to matter little in the first contest, as the Warriors looked completely out of sync. But they gained their legs, thanks in part to reserve Phil Smith, who netted 20 points. Meanwhile, Beard and Johnson bottled up Porter, and Golden State won 101-95.

With the series moving out West, Barry convinced his teammates that San Francisco's Cow Palace, not the Oakland Coliseum Arena, offered a better homecourt advantage, so Games 2 and 3 were booked into the new venue. The first night, the feisty forward backed up his words, pouring in 36 points in a thrilling 92-91 victory. Barry did it again in the next contest, recording a game-high 38 points as the Warriors won

109-101. For the shell-shocked Bullets, Game 4 was mostly about saving face and avoiding a sweep. Golden State, on the other hand, wanted to send a message. The contest started on a rough note when Attles was ejected after an argument in the first quarter. Washington proceeded to build a 14-point lead, but the Warriors battled back. Down the stretch, Beard scored the final seven points, including two clutch free throws, and Golden State capped its series upset, 96-95.

> **Warriors 4**
> **Bullets 0**
> **MVP: Rick Barry, Golden State**

1976
Boston Celtics vs. Phoenix Suns

In a year when no team distinguished itself as a finals favorite, the Boston Celtics rose above the Phoenix Suns in what turned out to be wildly entertaining finals. The Celtics were an aging group that didn't have many more title runs left in them. They got even older after trading young Paul Westphal to Phoenix for veteran Charlie Scott. The talented swingman combined with John Havlicek, Paul Silas, Dave Cowens, and Jo Jo White to form a starting five that coach Tom Heinsohn never seemed to take out of the game. All five averaged in double figures, making Boston very difficult to defend. The Celtics marched to the Atlantic Division crown with a record of 54-28. In the playoffs, the Celtics relied heavily on their homecourt advantage, defeating the Buffalo Braves and Cleveland Cavaliers in a pair of six-game series.

In Phoenix, the addition of Westphal paid big dividends. The ambidextrous shooting guard led the Suns in scoring and teamed with Dick Van Arsdale to form a solid backcourt. Along the front line, 6'9" center Alvan Adams loved to knock down jumpers from the perimeter. That opened things underneath for forwards Curtis Perry and Gar Heard, who was acquired from Buffalo in a midseason deal. Coach John MacLeod had tremendous confidence in his bench and used Ricky Sobers and Keith Erickson without hesitation. In fact, Sobers moved into the starting lineup when Van Arsdale broke his arm, and the hardnosed little guard stayed there throughout the playoffs. Phoenix went 42-40 during the regular season, good for third in the Pacific Division. The club then staged a pair of upsets, overcoming the Seattle Supersonics in the first round and the Golden State Warriors in the next to advance to the finals.

The Suns had not beaten the Celtics in the regular season, so many fans expected another four-game championship series. They appeared to be correct in Game 1 when, at the Boston Garden, Phoenix shot a dreadful 38 percent from the floor and lost 98-87. Not much changed in Game 2. In a 105-90 laugher, White was the star on offense, while Scott and Cowens played fabulous defense. The Suns returned home to Veterans Memorial Coliseum for Game 3 and decided not to let the Celtics bully them any longer. In Phoenix's 105-98 victory, Sobers set the tone early by engaging in a fight with Boston reserve Kevin Stacom. The refs put an end to the rough stuff in Game 4, whistling 21 fouls in the contest's first 10 minutes. When the action settled down, fans were treated to a thriller, which the Suns took, 109-107.

Game 5 in Boston proved to be one of the most exciting in NBA history. The Celtics threatened to blow out the Suns in the first quarter, but Phoenix cut the lead to 15 points at intermission. In the second half, they battled all the way back, tying the score at 95-95 in the last minute of the fourth quarter. The first overtime period ended with the game still knotted at 101-101, thanks to an oversight by the refs. With time running out, Silas signaled for a Boston timeout, even though his team had already used its quota. According to NBA rules, this should have been a technical foul, meaning the Suns were due a free throw. But the officials never saw Silas' signal, and the contest went into double-

overtime. In the next period, with Boston up by a point, the fans stormed onto the floor prematurely, as there was still one last tick on the clock. When the court was cleared, Phoenix intentionally took a technical foul, which would enable them to inbound the ball from halfcourt. Trailing 112-110 after the Celtics canned their free throw, Phoenix got the ball to Heard, who twirled and swished a high-arcing shot from more than 30 feet away to tie the game again. In the third overtime, Heinsohn was forced to go to the last man on his bench, a reserve named Glenn McDonald. The unknown forward miraculously scored 6 points to give the Celtics a dramatic 128-126 win. With both teams exhausted, Game 6 developed into a defensive struggle, which Boston took 87-80 to clinch its 13th NBA title. White, who averaged nearly 22 points, was voted MVP, but it was the incredible finish to Game 5 that people remembered most.

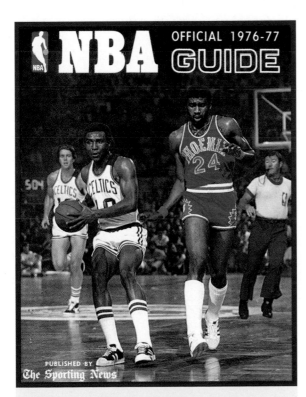

The heroics of Jo Jo White and Garfield Heard in the 1976 finals made them "cover boys" on the 1976-77 NBA Guide.

Celtics 4
Suns 2
MVP: Jo Jo White, Boston

1977
Philadelphia 76ers vs. Portland Trailblazers

After the 1975-76 season, the rival American Basketball Association folded its tent. The NBA absorbed four teams, but the rest of the ABA's talent was dispersed throughout pro basketball. Not surprisingly, the two teams that made the 1977 finals owed much to this infusion of talent.

The Trailblazers, a franchise originally created to keep the ABA out of basketball-crazy Portland, had struggled for several years thanks to mediocre talent and untimely injuries. Their luck began to change after the team drafted UCLA star Bill Walton. The multitalented center helped mold a group of smart, dedicated players into a consistent winner. Coach Jack Ramsey, an assistant with the 76ers when Wilt Chamberlain starred for them, understood the possibilities a player like Walton created. Not until the arrival of a big, nasty ABA power forward named Maurice Lucas, however, were the Blazers ready to take the next step. He and Walton led a club that included forward Bob

Bill Walton hungrily eyes a rebound. The Portland center introduced a new look to the NBA, but he won with old-time fundamentals.

Gross and Herm Gilliam and guards Dave Twardzik, Lionel Hollins, Larry Steele, and Johnny Davis. Portland finished second in the Pacific Division at 49-33. In the league's expanded playoff format, the Blazers beat the Chicago Bulls in a three-game series, raced by the Denver Nuggets 4 games to 2, and then swept the Los Angeles Lakers to reach the finals.

The Philadelphia 76ers were truly a creation of the ABA. They bought Julius Erving from the ABA's New York Nets, who needed to raise cash in order to enter the NBA. "Dr. J" was an acrobatic forward who turned the dunk into a cultural phenomenon. George McGinnis, a former ABA scoring champ and MVP, held down the other forward spot, while Caldwell Jones—who led the ABA in blocked shots—was the 76er center. Guards Doug Collins and Henry Bibby were NBA'ers, as was Lloyd Free who came off the bench for coach Gene Shue to provide instant offense. Forward Steve Mix, the team's star before Erving and friends came over, now served in a backup capacity. The 76ers rode their often undisciplined brilliance to first place in the Atlantic Division at 50-32. After a bye in the post-season's first round, they fended off the Boston Celtics in a tense seven-game series before eliminating the Houston Rockets in six games to earn a shot at Portland.

The Trailblazers opened Game 1 at Philadelphia's Spectrum looking ragged. Erving began the contest with a stupendous stuff, and Portland never recovered. With Dr. J tallying 33 points, the 76ers won 107-101. Philadelphia was even better in Game 2, surging to a 107-89 victory. The contest turned ugly late when Lucas and Darryl Dawkins, a hulking young center for the 76ers, ignited a bench-clearing brawl. The melee seemed to awaken Portland. At home in the Rose Garden for Games 3 and 4, the Trailblazers cruised to two easy wins. In the first, a 129-107 blowout, Walton did it all, registering 20 points, 18 rebounds, and 9 assists. The next night, the big redhead focused on defense, while Lucas pounded away on the offensive boards in a 130-98 rout.

Now on a roll, Portland returned to Philly and continued to pour it on. Thanks to a combined 69 points from Walton, Lucas, and Gross, the Trailblazers breezed to another win, 110-104. Portland was determined to end the series in Game 6. Leading by four points with less than a minute left, the Trailblazers appeared to be in command. But McGinnis canned one of his odd-looking one-handed jumpers and then forced a turnover that put the game up for grabs. The Trailblazers fended off three scoring attempts by Philadelphia and held on to win 109-107. Walton, the finals MVP, hurled his sweat-drenched jersey to his delirious fans. For perhaps the only time that season, the consummate team player basked for a moment in individual glory.

> Trailblazers 4
> 76ers 2
> MVP: Bill Walton, Portland

Wes Unseld scores in close for the Bullets. Though a half-foot shorter than many opposing centers, Unseld used positioning, anticipation, and his massive body to gain a competitive edge.

1978
Washington Bullets vs. Seattle Supersonics

Coming into the 1977-78 campaign, the Washington Bullets had the look of a team that time was passing by. The nucleus of Elvin Hayes, Wes Unseld, and Phil Chenier was aging, and some experts thought Washington no longer had the heart or desire to capture a title. But coach Dick Motta, a passionate taskmaster, saw tremendous potential in the Bullets—even when Chenier went down with a season-ending back injury. He inserted 24-year-old Kevin Grevey into the backcourt next to Tom Henderson, which gave his squad an infusion of youth. Up front he allowed Hayes and Bob Dandridge to freelance on offense, while Unseld conserved his energy and focused on the defensive end of the floor. When Motta needed a lift from the bench, he called upon

Mitch Kupchak, Larry Wright, and Charles Johnson. The Bullets finished second in the Central Division to the San Antonio Spurs with a record of 44-38. After a preliminary round sweep of the Atlanta Hawks, they surprised the Spurs and the 76ers in succession to earn a shot at a title.

Seattle also scored a couple of shockers on its march to the finals. Earlier in the year, the team wasn't responding to coach Bob Hopkins, so management replaced him with Lenny Wilkens. He got the starting five of John Johnson, Jack Sikma, Marvin Webster, Dennis Johnson, and Gus Williams to work together, and the Sonics took off. With rebounding whiz Paul Silas and marksman Fred Brown coming off the bench, Seattle won 42 of its last 60 games and was on a roll heading into the playoffs. The Sonics edged the Los Angeles Lakers before beating the Portland Trailblazers and Denver Nuggets.

The Bullets jumped out to a 19-point lead in Game 1 in Seattle, only to blow it in the second half when Brown got hot for the Sonics. With the long-bombing guard hitting for 16 in the contest's final 9 minutes, the home team came away with a 106-102 victory. Unseld wouldn't let his teammates hang their heads. When the series moved to Washington's Cap Center for Game 2, the burly center flexed his considerable muscle, controlling the boards and setting vicious picks for Hayes and Dandridge. His physical performance was the difference in Washington's 106-98 win. In Game 3, the Bullets hoped to make it two in a row on their home floor, but the Sonics won 93-92, thanks to a superb effort by Dennis Johnson. Back in Seattle for Game 4, the teams waged a terrific battle that went to overtime. In the extra period, Charles Johnson sparked Washington with three quick bas-

kets on the way to a 120-116 decision. The Sonics turned the tables in Game 5, as Brown and Johnson combined for 50 points in a 98-94 victory.

With their backs to the wall, the Bullets looked to be in trouble early in Game 6 when Grevey was injured and left the contest. Motta then gambled by moving Dandridge to guard and inserting forward Greg Ballard. To the delight of the fans at the Cap Centre, the switch worked perfectly, as Washington routed the Sonics, 117-82. Through the first three quarters of Game 7, Washington capitalized on awful shooting from the Sonics' starting backcourt to go up by 11 points. Webster and Sikma, however, helped Seattle cut that margin to four in the fourth quarter. With less than 2 minutes remaining and the Bullets leading 101-99, Unseld (a terrible free throw shooter) was fouled. He calmly sank his two attempts, and Washington held on for a 105-99 win that gave Washington the championship.

> **Bullets 4**
> **Supersonics 3**
> **MVP: Wes Unseld, Washington**

1979
Washington Bullets vs. Seattle Supersonics

The Seattle Supersonics could have thrown in the towel after their disappointing home loss to the Washington Bullets in Game 7 of the 1978 finals. The team retooled, however, and this time it finished the job. The backcourt tandem of Gus Williams and Dennis Johnson continued to be steady and often spectacular, as did super-sub Fred

Brown. John Johnson returned at forward, while Jack Sikma switched to center. Coach Lenny Wilkens tabbed youngster Lonnie Shelton—acquired from the Knicks in a deal for Marvin Webster—as the other starting forward, and veteran Paul Silas stuck around to provide valuable leadership. Seattle improved to 52-30 in the regular season to take the Pacific Division. In the playoffs, the Sonics handled the Los Angeles Lakers with ease before overcoming the Phoenix Suns in a tough seven-game series.

Emboldened by their championship, the Washington Bullets played with tremendous confidence throughout the 1978-79 campaign. Management handed coach Dick Motta virtually the exact same squad from the previous season, as Elvin Hayes, Bob Dandridge, and Wes Unseld remained upfront and Kevin Grevey and Tom Henderson started in the backcourt. Off the bench, Charles Johnson, Larry Wright, Mitch Kupchak, and Greg Ballard saw plenty of action, even in crunch time. The Bullets cruised to the top spot in the Atlantic Division with a record of 54-28. In the postseason, however, they were twice pushed to the limit, first by the Atlanta Hawks and then by the San Antonio Spurs.

In a rematch of the previous year's final, the Bullets seemed to hold the advantage, especially with the first two contests of the series at the Cap Centre. But Washington's players were clearly worn out. The Bullets escaped with a two-point victory in Game 1 when Wright was fouled with no time on the clock and the score tied The second-stringer calmly sank both free throws for a 99-97 win. Game 2 saw the Sonics turn up the defensive pressure on weary Washington and win easily, 92-82.

When the series shifted out West, Seattle turned up the heat. The home team opened Game 3 by hounding the Bullets all over the court. Up by 13 points after the first quarter, the Sonics never looked back in a 105-95 victory. Johnson was particularly effective with 17 points, nine rebounds, and two blocks. In Game 4, Washington tried to get even in an ugly contest that featured 59 fouls. Trailing by seven points late, the Bullets rallied to send the game to overtime. Led by their backcourt, the Sonics survived, 114-112, to seize control of the series. They closed it out in Washington, despite a brilliant game from Hayes. Brown gave Seattle a lift off the bench in the fourth quarter and the Sonics won, 97-93.

> **Supersonics 4**
> **Bullets 1**
> **MVP: Dennis Johnson, Seattle**

CHAPTER 4

THE 1980s

1980 Season
Philadelphia 76ers vs.
Los Angeles Lakers

Heading into the 1979-80 campaign the NBA was struggling. Enthusiasm for the pro game was waning, attendance was sagging, and several teams were uncomfortably close to bankruptcy. The league had more quality players than ever, but more and more the qualities of those players were coming under scrutiny. Fans were tired of reading about salary squabbles and other off-the-court problems, including a sharp rise in drug use. Television ratings for league games were so miserable that the 1979 NBA finals were aired on tape delay in some parts of the country. The NBA needed more than a savior. It needed two.

The season started with all eyes on a pair of rookies named Larry Bird and Magic Johnson. They had captured the basketball world's attention the previous April, when their college teams met at the NCAA championship. Now they were taking their show on the road in the NBA. Bird joined a Boston Celtic team in the doldrums after a nice run in the mid-1970s. Johnson slid right into a squad full of superstars. The outgoing and ebullient 6'9" point guard re-

vitalized a Los Angeles Laker club that featured aging Kareem Abdul-Jabbar, silky Jamaal Wilkes, and lightning-quick Norm Nixon. Behind this group was a talented bench that included Jim Chones, Michael Cooper, and Spencer Haywood. Early in the season, coach Jack McKinney was injured in a cycling accident. His replacement, Paul Westhead, let the 20-year-old Magic do his thing and watched as Los Angeles fashioned a 60-22 record. In the playoffs, the Lakers dumped the Phoenix Suns and Seattle Supersonics with ease.

The league desperately wanted the season to end with a Bird-Johnson match-up in the finals, but the Philadelphia 76ers spoiled the party. Coach Billy Cunningham, a member of Philly's 1967 championship team, built his team on the brilliant scoring of Julius Erving, tough defense and good rebounding. Dr. J averaged 26.9 points a night, with many of his buckets coming on eye-popping dunks. The rest of the starting cast—forward Bobby Jones, center Darryl Dawkins, and guards Doug Collins and Maurice Cheeks—were blue-collar workers who dove for loose balls and weren't afraid to take a charge. Philadelphia got more of the same from its bench, which included familiar faces Caldwell Jones, Henry Bibby, and Steve Mix. Even when Collins was sidelined with a knee injury, the 76ers found the perfect replacement in Lionel Hollins, acquired in a trade from the Portland Trailblazers. Despite a record of 59-23, Philly was edged out for first in the Atlantic Division by Bird and the Celtics. The 76ers worked their way past the Bullets and Hawks in the playoffs, then beat the Celtics twice on their home turf in playoffs to earn a berth in the NBA finals.

Los Angeles opened the finals at home in the Forum on the right note, winning Game 1 by a score of 109-102. Abdul-Jabbar was the key, recording 33 points, 14 rebounds, and six blocks, while Johnson finished with 16 points and nine assists. The 76ers looked to Erving to rally them in Game 2, and he responded with 23 points in a 107-104 victory. Philadelphia almost blew the comfortable lead in the waning moments, but Bobby Jones saved them with a clutch jumper. When the series moved to the Spectrum in Philly for Game 3, Abdul-Jabbar made his presence felt again, posting another 33-point performance in a 111-101 win. In Game 4, the 76ers benefited from a big night by the irrepressible Dawkins, who decided to start firing 20-footers and ended up scoring 26 points. The highlight of the game was a baseline drive by Erving, who floated past Mark Landsberger and Abdul-Jabbar, continued past the basket, then flicked the ball in before he landed out of bounds. The Doctor's gravity-defying shot was all anyone could talk about after Philadelphia's series-tying 105-102 victory.

Back home for Game 5, Laker fortunes sank even further when their center suffered a badly sprained ankle. His teammates hung tough, however, and Abdul-Jabbar limped back on the court in the final quarter to

Julius Erving finishes one of the most famous shots in NBA history. His soaring reverse layup stunned Laker defenders Mark Landsberger and Kareem Abdul-Jabbar.

score the winning basket in a 108-103 victory. The series headed back to Philadelphia, by which time team doctors had determined that Kareem would be unavailable the rest of the way. Westhead thought long and hard about a suitable replacement, and the only guy he could come up with was his 20-year-old point guard. He was tall enough to hold his own against Dawkins and Caldwell Jones, and energetic enough to keep them huffing and puffing. No one, not even Magic, could have imagined what happened next. The rookie took the

Philadelphia big men completely out of their games, and whirled and twirled his way to 42 points and 15 rebounds. The Lakers snuffed out several 76er rallies and triumphed 123-107 to win the championship.

> Lakers 4
> 76ers 2
> MVP: Magic Johnson, Los Angeles

1981
Boston Celtics vs. Houston Rockets

As the final buzzer sounded on their playoff loss to the 76ers, in the spring of 1980, the Celtics looked like a team about to embark on a rebuilding program. They had their cornerstone in Larry Bird, the NBA's Rookie of the Year. But center Dave Cowens was retiring, guard Nate Archibald was on the downside of his career, and the rest of the club—including Cornbread Maxwell, Chris Ford, Gerald Henderson and M.L. Carr—looked pretty ordinary. In what has to be the fastest rebuilding program in history, GM Red Auerbach pulled off a draft-day coup, sending his team's two first-round picks to the Warriors for one pick and an underachieving center named Robert Parish. Auerbach then spent his pick on gangly Kevin McHale, a player who seemed too slight to play a power position in the NBA, and too awkward to play anywhere else. Sixty-two wins later, Bird had become the NBA's ultimate go-to guy, Parish, McHale, and Maxwell played defense like a brick wall, and Ford and Archibald were making things happen in the backcourt. Coach Bill Fitch blended his

talent masterfully right through the playoffs, as Boston swept the Chicago Bulls and then shocked Philadelphia in seven games.

Once again, Bird and Johnson did not meet in the finals. This time around the Houston Rockets ruined the fun. Coached by Del Harris, the Rockets finished at a mediocre 40-42, good for a second place tie in the Midwest Division. It wasn't that Houston was devoid of talent, however. Their center, Moses Malone, was relentless under the boards and an unstoppable scorer when he got the ball near the basket. 5'9" Calvin Murphy darted around the court like a water bug, drawing fouls, setting up teammates, and exhausting rival guards. His backcourt mate, Mike Dunleavy, and reserves Allen Leavell and Tom Henderson, were good playmakers and solid defenders. At forward, Robert Reid, Rudy Tomjanovich, Billy Paultz, and Calvin Garrett all shared playing time, with Reid the best of the bunch. In the post-season, the Rockets came alive and upended the Lakers in the opening round. They used the momentum from that series to take the next two against the San Antonio Spurs and Kansas City Kings.

Armed with the home court advantage, the Celtics figured to coast through the finals, but Game 1 was tense from the opening tip. With Houston ahead in the fourth quarter, Bird made the play of the game, following his own miss of an 18-foot jumper with an incredible put-back. The bucket energized the Boston Garden crowd and sparked the Celtics to a 98-95 win. Surprisingly, Boston came out flat in the Game 2. Despite Fitch's attempts to motivate his squad, the Rockets controlled the tempo and stunned the Celtics 92-90. Game 3 in the Houston Summit was all Boston. With the pesky Maxwell—a thorn in Houston's side throughout the series—leading the way on both ends, the Celtics routed the Rockets 94-71.

Del Harris decided to shake things up in Game 4, ignoring his bench and using only six players. Houston responded with a 91-86 victory. Afterwards, Malone bragged loudly, contending that Boston wasn't all that good. The Celtics read his comments in the papers and vowed to make him pay. In Game 5 in Boston, they throttled the Rockets, 109-80. Two nights later, Boston ended the series in Houston with a 102-91 win. In the locker room, Bird took a puff of Red Auerbach's cigar and yelled, "We're the champions."

Celtics 4
Rockets 2
MVP: Cornbread Maxwell, Boston

1982
Philadelphia 76ers vs. Los Angeles Lakers

For the third straight year Magic Johnson and Larry Bird did not meet as expected in the finals. Still, the NBA was beginning to win back fans because of their rivalry. The league was getting smarter about its image, and was beginning to develop a new generation of media-savvy superstars led by these two great young players. After being embarrassed by Houston in the playoffs, the Lakers vowed to make it back to the finals in 1982. So serious was Johnson about this goal that he orchestrated a revolt against coach Paul Westhead, whom he felt was not fully developing the team's talents. Management sided with Magic, and former Laker sub Pat Riley was hired as the new

coach. Riley had a lot to work with. The nucleus of Johnson, Kareem Abdul-Jabbar, Jamaal Wilkes, and Norm Nixon remained intact. When forward Mitch Kupchak hurt his knee, Riley increased playing time for Michael Cooper, Mark Landsberger, Kurt Rambis, Jim Brewer, and Bob McAdoo. Los Angeles sprinted to first place in the Pacific Division with a record of 57-25 on the strength of its "Showtime" fast-break offense. In the playoffs, the team swept the Phoenix Suns and San Antonio Spurs.

The Philadelphia 76ers finished second to the Celtics, but the teams were very close in terms of talent. Coach Billy Cunningham made Caldwell Jones a starter and used Darryl Dawkins off the bench, and promoted young Andrew Toney to first-string. The incomparable Julius Erving continued to star up front alongside the ever-consistent Bobby Jones. Maurice Cheeks ran the team without error from the point, while Lionel Hollins was always good for a clutch basket off the bench. Despite a record of 58-24, the 76ers couldn't catch the Celtics in the Atlantic Division. Philly waltzed by the Atlanta Hawks in the postseason's preliminary round, before first facing stiff challenges from the Milwaukee Bucks, whom they beat in six games. In a battle with the Celtics, Philly prevailed in seven games for a return trip to the finals.

The finals opened at the Spectrum in Philadelphia with the well-rested Lakers springing a new defense on the 76ers. Thought the 76ers led in the second half, Los Angeles went on a 40-9 run to win 124-117. In Game 2, Dr. J stepped up with 24 points and 16 rebounds. His performance, combined with a solid defensive effort against Abdul-Jabbar, gave Philadelphia a 110-94 victory. Games 3 & 4 at the Forum in Los Angeles demonstrated the Lakers' tremendous versatility. The first night they used high-pressure defense to fuel their high-octane running game and race to a 129-108 win. In the next contest, Los Angeles slowed it down, as Johnson, Wilkes, and Abdul-Jabbar combined for 70 points in a 111-101 victory.

Philadelphia made a stand in Game 5 at the Spectrum. Holding Abdul-Jabbar to just six points, the 76ers routed the Lakers 135-102. Game 6 offered Johnson and his teammates the opportunity to capture the title on their home floor. Up by 9 points at intermission, Los Angeles refused to falter in the second half. After Philadelphia cut the deficit in the fourth quarter, Johnson took over and Riley's troops held on to win 114-104. Johnson's timely play earned him another MVP trophy, though he was the first to admit that this title was a total team effort.

> Lakers 4
> 76ers 2
> MVP: Magic Johnson, Los Angeles

Moses Malone eyes the rim from the front of his 1981-82 Topps trading card. What better place to show the Houston center than on the foul line, where he scored a third of his points?

1983
Philadelphia 76ers vs.
Los Angeles Lakers

After losing to the Los Angeles Lakers in the finals twice in the previous three years, the Philadelphia 76ers knew exactly what they needed to get them over the hump. Philly had fallen because they couldn't match Kareem Abdul-Jabbar at center. The team took care of that problem by unloading Caldwell Jones and Darryl Dawkins and replacing them with free agent Moses Malone, who worked harder than any other center in the league. Malone fit in perfectly

with forwards Julius Erving and Bobby Jones and guards Maurice Cheeks and Andrew Toney. Coach Billy Cunningham looked to guard Clint Richardson, forward Marc Iavaroni, and center Clemon Johnson off the bench when one of his starters needed a rest. From the regular season's opening day, the 76ers and their fans sensed this was their year. Philadelphia powered to a record of 65-17, good for first in the Atlantic Division. On its way to the finals, the club dropped only 1 game, sweeping the New York Knicks and then handling the Milwaukee Bucks in five games.

The Lakers hoped to defend their title by relying on a proven formula. Magic Johnson, who ran the show from the point, and Kareem Abdul-Jabbar, still an offensive machine, anchored the NBA's most potent attack. Complementing them was the outside shooting of Jamaal Wilkes and the all-around game of Norm Nixon. When rookie James Worthy joined the starting five, coach Pat Riley had a club that could beat opponents inside, outside, and on the break. Also figuring into the mix was the explosive Bob McAdoo and defensive specialists Kurt Rambis and Michael Cooper. After taking first place in the Pacific Division at 58-24, the Lakers began the post-season by breezing past the Portland Trailblazers. In the next round, they outplayed the San Antonio Spurs to earn a rematch with the 76ers.

Los Angeles was a battered group when entering the finals. Worthy was out with a broken left leg suffered at the end of the regular season. Nixon and McAdoo both got injured in the playoffs and the status of each was questionable. The 76ers welcomed the opportunity to pounce on their wounded opponent. In Game 1 at the Spectrum, the Lakers raced to a halftime lead only to see Philly charge back even harder to easily win 113-107. Game 2 followed an identical script, as the 76ers again dominated in the second half on the way to a 103-93 victory. In both games, Malone controlled the paint, Abdul-Jabbar simply could not match his intensity and strength. The rout continued when the series moved to the Forum in Los Angeles. With Nixon limping on a sore left knee in Game 3, the Lakers were blown out by a score of 111-94.

Philadelphia was eager to finish off Los Angeles in Game 4, but the home team put up a good fight. Midway through the fourth

quarter, the Lakers seemed to be in control with a 2-point lead. That's when Erving announced to his teammates that he was "taking over." Dr. J stole a pass and dunked to tie the contest. He canned another shot and was fouled for a 3-point play. Then he drained a jumper in Magic's face. The 76ers never trailed again, cruising to a 115-108 win and the franchise's second NBA title. Malone was the deserving choice as MVP, though it was three shots from the Doctor that clinched the series.

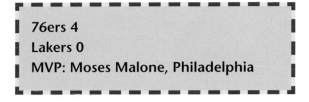

76ers 4
Lakers 0
MVP: Moses Malone, Philadelphia

1984
Boston Celtics vs. Los Angeles Lakers

NBA fans finally got their wish in the spring of 1984 when Larry Bird and Magic Johnson led their teams to the finals. Bird had been an All-Star since his rookie year and captured a title in 1981, but it wasn't until Red Auerbach made several key moves that the Boston Celtics established themselves as the class of the East. First he hired K.C. Jones, one of his old players, as coach. Then he traded center Rick Robey to Phoenix for guard Dennis Johnson. Jones's laidback style and Johnson's veteran savvy made the Celtics almost unbeatable. Boston's greatest strength remained its frontcourt. Bird, Cornbread Maxwell, and Robert Parish were a devastating trio, and Kevin McHale was just incredible off the bench. Johnson and Gerald Henderson were a well-matched tandem, though Jones also

Larry Bird splits the defense and drives to the basket. He and Magic Johnson rekindled fan interest at a time when NBA fortunes were sagging.

worked Quinn Buckner, Danny Ainge, Scott Wedman, and M.L. Carr into the backcourt rotation. The Celtics won the Atlantic Division with surprising ease at 62-20. In the playoffs, they had no problem with the Washington Bullets in the first round, but Bernard King and the New York Knicks gave them a seven-game scare in the next. Boston then found its rhythm against the Milwaukee Bucks to reach the finals.

In Los Angeles, general manager Jerry

West added youth to the team by acquiring 22-year-old guard Byron Scott from the San Diego Clippers for Norm Nixon. That trade moved Michael Cooper into the starting lineup next to Magic and put more scoring onus on forward James Worthy. Both settled into their roles nicely. Kareem Abdul-Jabbar, who passed Wilt Chamberlain as the NBA's all-time leading scorer, was magnificent at center, while Jamaal Wilkes remained steady as ever at forward. Johnson, who dished out 13 assists a game, made everything go with his wonderful passing. Coach Pat Riley wasn't afraid to call on his bench, either. Bob McAdoo and Mike McGee were his top gunners, but when Wilkes suffered a stomach infection late in the season, rugged Kurt Rambis became a starter. The Lakers won the Pacific Division with a record of 54-28 and then took off in the playoffs. They swept the Kansas City Kings, defeated the Dallas Mavericks in 5 games, and beat the Phoenix Suns in 6.

Excitement was at a fever pitch heading into Game 1 at the Boston Garden. Abdul-Jabbar, was bothered by a migraine headache so intense that it nearly kept him on the sidelines. But the 7'2" center played despite the pain and turned out to be the hero with 32 points and 8 rebounds in a 115-109 victory. Thanks to an offensive outburst by Worthy, the Lakers looked like they would take Game 2 as well. With 18 seconds left, however, Henderson converted a layup after a steal to send the contest into overtime. In the extra period, Wedman surprised the Lakers by canning a clutch shot that fueled Boston's 124-121 win.

It was "Showtime" in Game 3 at the Forum in Los Angeles. With Johnson piling up a record 21 assists, the Lakers ran past the Celtics 137-104. Jones switched gears in

Game 4 and assigned Denis Johnson the task of guarding Magic. The move slowed down the Los Angeles fast break a bit, but more important was Boston's rough-and-tough attitude. Late in the fourth quarter, the Celtics forced overtime with a combination of physical defense and clutch shooting. When Worthy missed a key foul shot in OT, Boston held on 129-125. The Celtics now believed they could intimidate the Lakers— a tactic they employed the rest of the way. They also felt Bird was due for a big night. He responded in Game 5 back at the Boston Garden with a 34-point outburst. His masterful performance, which included 15-of-20 shooting from the floor, was the story in the 121-103 rout by the Celtics. The Lakers stood their ground in Game 6 in Los Angeles. Early in the contest, Worthy set the tone by shoving Maxwell under the boards. Abdul-Jabbar took it from there, scoring 30 points as the Lakers won 119-108.

Game 7 attracted the league's largest television audience to date. Maxwell sparked the Celtics with a variety of shots in the paint that either fell through the hoop or drew a referee's whistle. Down by 14 points in the second half, Los Angeles climbed back into the game. With a minute remaining, Magic spotted Worthy underneath the basket, but Maxwell tipped away the pass, and the Celtics regained their composure. Their 111-102 win gave Boston its 15th championship. The series everyone so desperately wanted to see was even better than anticipated. And the best was yet to come!

Celtics 4
Lakers 3
MVP: Larry Bird, Boston

1985
Boston Celtics vs. Los Angeles Lakers

Thanks to the thrilling 1984 finals between the Los Angeles Lakers and Boston Celtics, the NBA was experiencing a tremendous resurgence with fans. The league's popularity rose further when Michael Jordan hit the scene. But the rookie guard and his Chicago Bulls were a few years away from challenging for a championship. Still seething from their seven-game loss the year before, the Lakers wanted revenge. Coach Pat Riley had his team ready from the get-go. Magic Johnson was the NBA's most difficult

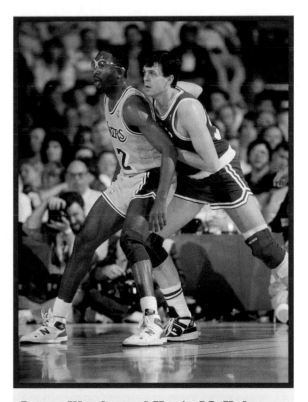

James Worthy and Kevin McHale battle for position. These great forwards did all the "little things" that translated into championships.

TEAM SPIRIT
THE 1980s:
BOSTON CELTICS AND LOS ANGELES LAKERS

NBA fans were treated to two wonderful teams during the 1980s, the Los Angeles Lakers and Boston Celtics. Each club featured a high-profile superstar obsessed with making his teammates better and surrounded with other All-Stars and future Hall-of-Famers. Not surprisingly, whenever the Lakers and Celtics played, it was an athletic event of the highest order.

The Lakers were led by Magic Johnson, the 6'9" playmaking guard whose sparkling smile masked the heart of a basketball assassin. Johnson looked for an opponent's vulnerability, then exploited it without mercy. He was aided by aging Kareem Abdul-Jabbar, who rediscovered his youthful enthusiasm with Magic running the team, and forward James Worthy, who could bang the boards and run the floor with equal effectiveness.

Under coach Pat Riley, the Lakers learned how to play two games. The first—which he called "Showtime"—was the glamorous transition game that featured lots of fast breaks, alley-oops, and slam dunks. The second—which became crucial come playoff time—was a precise, halfcourt offense that relied more on the skills of their inside players, especially Abdul-Jabbar and James Worthy.

The Lakers reached the NBA Finals eight times during the decade, and three times their opponents were the Celtics. Boston's team was built around forward Larry Bird, who controlled games with his clutch scoring and brilliant passing. Bird played 1960s-style ball with 1980s-style attitude, and he was surrounded by a group of tough, hard-working teammates, including center Robert Parish, forward Kevin McHale, and guard Dennis Johnson.

The Celtics reached the finals five times between 1981 and 1987. Red Auerbach, who still ran the team, never lost his talent for finding players to fit the system. He also chose his coaches wisely, bringing in Bill Fitch to reshape the club in the early 1980s, then replacing him with Boston legend K.C. Jones, who won two championships in his first three years on the Celtic sidelines.

What the two teams had in common, besides a deep respect for each other, was a knack for finding exactly the right kind of players to support their stars. Some had been All-Stars themselves in the past—like Celtics Nate Archibald and Bill Walton, and Lakers Bob McAdoo and Spencer Haywood—while others excelled in specific areas that won championships, like Boston's Danny Ainge and L.A.'s Byron Scott and Michael Cooper, who had a talent for hitting from the perimeter. It is worth noting that no player played for both teams during this era.

player to defend. At 37, Kareem Abdul-Jabbar kept on chugging along. And James Worthy matured into a star. Meanwhile, Riley inserted Kurt Rambis and Byron Scott into the starting lineup, and both proved to be valuable contributors. Michael Cooper offered great defense off the bench, while Jamaal Wilkes, Bob McAdoo, and Mike McGee chipped in with important points in their reserve roles. Los Angeles fashioned a 62-20 record, taking the Pacific Division by 20 games. In the post-season, the Lakers destroyed the Phoenix Suns, Portland Trailblazers, and Denver Nuggets to advance to the finals.

The Celtics were equally dominant in the East. Like Riley, coach K.C. Jones fiddled with his starting five, replacing Cedric Maxwell with Kevin McHale and Cedric Henderson with Danny Ainge. The team's leader was still Larry Bird, who claimed his second regular-season MVP award in a row. Robert Parish enjoyed another solid campaign at center, and guard Dennis Johnson provided his usual timely scoring and excellent defense. Maxwell accepted his reserve role without complaint, while Scott Wedman continued to supply important points off the bench. Boston's record of 63-19 was tops in the league. The Celtics then marched through their playoff series with the Cleveland Cavaliers, Detroit Pistons, and Philadelphia 76ers.

The hype leading up to the finals was amazing. The NBA's two premier players, Magic and Bird, were back at it, as Los Angeles and Boston prepared to add a new chapter to the league's fiercest rivalry. Game 1, since dubbed the "Memorial Day Massacre," only fueled the fire as the Celtics routed the Lakers 148-114. Wedman scored 26 points, hitting all 11 of his shots

from the floor, including four 3-pointers. The embarrassed Lakers regrouped in Game 2, placing more emphasis on defense. With Abdul-Jabbar asserting himself with 30 points and 17 rebounds, Los Angeles silenced the Boston faithful, 109-102. Riley's troops returned home feeling confident, especially since the next three contests were at the Forum. In Game 3, they engineered a 136-111 blowout, as Abdul-Jabbar and Worthy combined for 55 points.

Down 2-1, the Celtics needed a win to keep the series from getting away from

Kareem Abdul-Jabbar's unstoppable sky hook. This weapon enabled him to dominate big games, as he did against the Celtics in the 1985 finals.

them. With the minutes dwindling in Game 4 and the score knotted 105-105, Bird passed out of a double-team to Johnson, who knocked down a jumper for a dramatic win. In Game 5, Riley discovered that Abdul-Jabbar was a stronger force against McHale and Rambis against Parish. The switch worked beautifully as the Lakers ran away from the Celtics 120-111. Los Angeles now needed just one win to settle the score with Boston. The plan going into Game 6 was to feed the ball to Abdul-Jabbar. But foul trouble kept him on the bench in the second quarter, and the score at intermission was tied. In the second half, however, Kareem netted 18 points, spearheading a charge that lifted Los Angeles to a 111-100 win and the NBA title. The Lakers had waited for more than 20 years to beat the Celtics in the post-season. Their victory was especially sweet, as it came on Boston's hallowed parquet floor.

Lakers 4
Celtics 2
MVP: Kareem Abdul-Jabbar, Los Angeles

1986
Boston Celtics vs. Houston Rockets

Red Auerbach knew his team was good enough to reclaim the title, so the Boston GM tinkered with his roster only slightly. He added reserves Bill Walton and Jerry Sichting, but the starting five didn't change at all. Larry Bird, Kevin McHale, and Robert Parish, together, averaged more than 60 points and nearly 30 rebounds a game. In the backcourt, Dennis Johnson and Danny Ainge were pesky defenders who had a knack for hitting big shots. During the regular season, Jones used his bench liberally, and Boston responded with a record of 67-15, its best mark ever. In the playoffs, the Celtics swept Michael Jordan and his Chicago Bulls, and then crushed the Atlanta Hawks and Milwaukee Bucks to reach the finals for the third year in a row.

The Houston Rockets surprised everyone in the West by advancing to the finals. With former Boston coach Bill Fitch at the helm, the Rockets were built around the twin towers of Hakeem Olajuwon and Ralph Sampson, a pair of 7-footers who offered a devastating 1-2 punch. Rodney McCray, Lewis Lloyd, Robert Reid, and Jim Petersen shared time along the frontline and in the backcourt. At the point, John Lucas was the team's floor leader, but when off-the-court problems landed him in drug rehabilitation, Fitch had to scramble to find a replacement. Ultimately, he moved Reid into the starting lineup and gave more minutes to reserve Mitchell Wiggins. Houston managed to win the the Midwest Division with a record of 51-31, then sped through the post-season's first two rounds, defeating the Sacramento Kings and the Denver Nuggets. In the Western Conference finals, the Rockets stunned the Lakers with a decisive, five-game victory.

Bird did it all on offense for the Celtics in Game 1, as Boston shot a sizzling 66 percent from the floor to take a 112-100 victory. Game 2 featured another heavy dose of Bird, who netted 31 points, while Boston continued to frustrate Olajuwon with its double-teaming defense. Thanks to a strong run in the third quarter, the Celtics scored a 117-95 win. When the series shifted to the Houston Summit, the Rockets hoped to find a way to get back in the series. Fitch hit upon a good plan in Game 4 when he asked Reid to shadow Bird. The move changed the momentum in the second half, and Houston rallied to eke out a 106-104 win. The Rockets, however, could only keep Bird down for so long. With time running out in the fourth quarter of Game 4, the Boston forward nailed a long 3-pointer to lift the Celtics to a 106-103 victory and give them a 3 games to 1 lead.

In Game 5, Sampson sparked his teammates with a fistfight that got him ejected. The Rockets rallied to beat the Celtics 111-96 and send the series back to Boston. Happy to be home, Bird seized control of Game 6 from the opening tip and never let go. The Celtics had a 15-point lead at the half and extended it to 30 in the fourth quarter. In the 114-97 shellacking, Bird finished with 29 points, 11 rebounds, and 12 assists. His fine performance throughout the postseason was the key to Boston's 16th NBA title.

> Celtics 4
> Rockets 2
> MVP: Larry Bird, Boston

1987
Boston Celtics vs. Los Angeles Lakers

Kareem Abdul-Jabbar was 39 years old heading into the 1986-87 campaign. If the Los Angeles Lakers were going to return to the NBA finals, they would need someone else to shoulder the scoring burden. Magic Johnson responded with a monster year, pushing his average to 23.9 points a game and becoming the first guard since Oscar Robertson in 1964 to be the MVP for the regular season. John-

son's teammates weren't so bad, either. James Worthy was now a bona fide All-Star, Byron Scott developed into a reliable scorer next to Magic, and second-year forward A.C. Green was the scrappy fifth member of Pat Riley's starting unit. In addition, the aging Abdul-Jabbar was still a force, though back-up Mychal Thompson made sure he didn't have to log too many minutes. Michael Cooper also continued to provide valuable contributions off the bench. Los Angeles stormed to first place in the Pacific Division with a record of 65-17. The Lakers had an easy time of it in the playoffs, losing just one game against the Denver Nuggets, Golden State Warriors, and Seattle Supersonics.

The Boston Celtics were beginning to feel the effects of age as well. Coach K.C. Jones's crew took the Atlantic Division again, this time with a 59-23 mark. But the team's health was an issue entering the postseason. Kevin McHale, who enjoyed the finest year of his career, was nursing a broken foot and Robert Parish had sprained an ankle. Fortunately, Larry Bird, Dennis Johnson, and Danny Ainge were all free from injury. Unlike the previous year, when everyone got into the act, Jones used his bench infrequently in 1986-87. Besides guard Jerry Sichting, no Celtic reserve ever made much of an impact. Boston's lack of depth roved a challenge in the playoffs. After sweeping the Chicago Bulls, the Celtics were pushed to brink by the Milwaukee Bucks and Detroit Pistons. The strain of going seven games in two consecutive series in a row definitely took its toll.

The finals opened in the Forum with the Lakers ready to pounce. In the first half alone, Los Angeles ran its vaunted fast break 35 times—a pace the tired Celtics simply couldn't maintain. In his team's

Magic Johnson blows past his man to the basket. Johnson's ability to penetrate enemy defenses created scoring opportunities for everyone on the Lakers.

win it. As the clock wound down, Magic lofted a hook shot over Parish that hit nothing but the bottom net for a stunning 107-106 win. In Game 5, Boston delayed the inevitable with a 123-108 win. Back home at the Forum, however, the Lakers would not be denied. With Magic again leading the way, Los Angeles cruised 106-93 for its fourth title of the decade.

Lakers 4
Celtics 2
MVP: Magic Johnson, Los Angeles

1988
Detroit Pistons vs. Los Angeles Lakers

Despite several "mini-dynasties" in the 1970s and 80s, no team had repeated as NBA champion since the Boston Celtics in 1969. Pat Riley, coach of the Los Angeles Lakers, was obsessed with ending that streak and knew he had the team to do it. By all accounts, Magic Johnson was the league's best player. His backcourt mate, Byron Scott, had improved to become the club's leading scorer. Along the front line, James Worthy was playing with tremendous confidence, A.C. Green filled his role as a strong defender and rebounder, and Kareem Abdul-Jabbar still showed flashes of greatness. Mychal Thompson and Michael Cooper remained Riley's top subs, while late-season pickup Tony Campbell gave the Lakers a proven scorer off the bench. Los Angeles took another Pacific Division crown with a record of 62-20, then swept by the San Antonio Spurs in the opening round of the playoffs. But both the Utah Jazz and

126-113 laugher, Magic posted 29 points and 13 assists. In Game 2, Boston planned to put the clamps on Johnson and keep the ball out of his hands. The Los Angeles point guard made his presence felt nonetheless, racking up 22 assists in another blowout, 141-122. The Celtics returned home battered but not beaten. In Game 3 at the Boston Garden, a 109-103 win by the home team, McHale ignored the pain in his foot and recorded 21 points and 10 rebounds.

Feeling more confident, Boston looked like a different team in Game 4. With less than 4 minutes remaining, the Celtics nursed an 8-point lead. But the Lakers fought back and went ahead 104-103. Bird nailed a 3-pointer to put Boston back on top. After Abdul-Jabbar sunk a free throw, the Lakers were given one more chance to

Dallas Mavericks extended the Lakers to seven games before acquiescing.

In the East, the Detroit Pistons broke the Celtic stranglehold on the conference with a deep squad of tough, focused role players led by their star point guard, Isiah Thomas. A terrific ballhandler, penetrator, passer, scorer, and defender, Thomas was capable of controlling games for several minutes at a time. Joining him in the backcourt were defensive genius Joe Dumars and Vinnie Johnson, nicknamed the "Microwave" for his ability to heat up off the bench. Forward Adrian Dantley was the Pistons' top scorer, but it was the other members of Detroit's front line who struck real fear into opponents. Rick Mahorn, Bill Laimbeer, Dennis Rodman, and John Salley formed a maze of elbows, hips, knees and other painful body parts that enemy players had to wade through whenever they got near the hoop. Detroit captured the Central Division crown at 54-28 and then launched an impressive postseason run. After surviving a scare from the Washington Bullets, the Pistons manhandled the Chicago Bulls and advanced to the finals by dethroning the Boston Celtics.

The series got off to a strange start at the Forum as off-court buddies Johnson and Thomas pecked each other on the cheek before the opening tap in Game 1. Dantley, however, delivered a blow right to the kisser of Los Angeles, hitting 14 of 16 shots in a 105-93 victory. Suddenly looking old, the Lakers taught their brash, young opponent a thing or two in Game 2. Thanks to 26 points from Worthy and 23 from Johnson (who played despite a bout with the flu) Los Angeles evened the series with a 108-96 win. When the action shifted to the Silverdome in Detroit, the Lakers were eager to make a statement in enemy territory. They did so

with a solid 99-86 victory. Green was the surprise offensive hero with 21 points. In Game 4, Piston coach Chuck Daly gave the Lakers a new look, as Rodman drew the assignment of guarding Magic. The long-limbed, trash-talking forward responded with a brilliant performance, sparking the Pistons 111-86. Game 5 in Detroit began with Los Angeles scoring the contest's first 12 points. But Dantley and Johnson rallied the Pistons to a 9-point lead at intermission. When Dumars picked up the slack in the second half, the home team breezed 104-94.

Down 3-2 in the series, the Lakers had their backs against the wall in Game 6. They led 56-48 at the half, but Thomas erupted for 25 points in the third quarter, 11 of which came after he suffered a painful sprained ankle. Los Angeles battled back on a clutch jumper by Scott with less than a minute left, and regained the lead on two free throws by Abdul-Jabbar. When Dumars missed a shot at the buzzer, Los Angeles had knotted the series and forced a seventh game. Thomas, who arrived in the locker room on crutches, started Game 7 and played well in the opening minutes, but then slowed in the second half. Worthy stepped up for the Lakers, and led them on a run that produced a 15-point lead. Detroit mounted a comeback, getting as close as 102-100, but Los Angeles held on to win 108-105 and defend its title. Worthy, who posted 36 points, 16 rebounds, and 10 assists in the clincher, was named MVP, while Riley was heralded as the emotional force behind his team's historic championship.

Lakers 4
Pistons 3
MVP: James Worthy, Los Angeles

1989
Detroit Pistons vs.
Los Angeles Lakers

The Detroit Pistons used their narrow loss to the Lakers in 1988 as motivation during the 1988-89 campaign. Coach Chuck Daly's troops raised their special brand of thuggery to an art form, and played just enough real basketball to win 63 games. Isiah Thomas and Joe Dumars teamed up in the league's best backcourt, while Vinnie Johnson bombed away whenever he came off the bench. Rick Mahorn, Bill Laimbeer, Dennis Rodman, and John Salley—now known on banners and t-shirts as the "Bad Boys"—continued to bully opponents. Midway through the season, the Pistons added another important puzzle piece when they shipped Adrian Dantley to the Dallas Mavericks in a trade for Mark Aguirre. Dantley had often annoyed the Pistons by griping that he didn't see the ball often enough. Aguirre, a burly forward who learned his game in the Chicago schoolyards, was a better fit in the Detroit locker room. In the playoffs, the team played at an even higher level, blowing past the Boston Celtics, Milwaukee Bucks, and Chicago Bulls.

The Lakers tried to match the Pistons every step of the way. When Kareem Abdul-Jabbar publicly announced he would retire at the end of the season, the Los Angeles center enjoyed an emotional farewell tour as fans around the league saluted his amazing career. Meanwhile, Magic Johnson added another MVP award to his trophy case, and James Worthy averaged more than 20 points a game for the first time in his career. Filling out the starting five were sharp-shooting Byron Scott and hardworking A.C. Green. Coach Pat Riley remained loyal to his two

Kareem Abdul-Jabbar launches a shot over Detroit's Rick Mahorn. The 1989 finals marked the last appearance of the NBA's all-time leading scorer.

top reserves, Mychal Thompson and Michael Cooper, and welcomed Orlando Woolridge, an offensive-minded veteran. The Lakers faced a stiff test from the Phoenix Suns during the regular season, but held them off to take the Pacific Division crown with 57 wins. Their postseason run was as impressive as Detroit's. Indeed, Los Angeles won 11 straight over the Portland Trailblazers, Seattle Supersonics, and

Phoenix to set up what most expected to be a terrific match-up against the Pistons.

Emotions ran high as the series began. The Lakers hoped to send Abdul-Jabbar out as a champion, while the Pistons were looking for payback from the year before. However, Los Angeles was not at full strength. Scott, L.A.'s sharpshooting guard, would not be available for the series due to a bad hamstring. In Game 1, the Pistons used their advantage in the backcourt to confound the Lakers. With Thomas, Dumars, and Johnson combining for 65 points, Detroit dismantled Los Angeles 109-97. In Game 2, the Lakers came out smoking, but Dumars netted 24 points in the first half to keep his team within striking range. By the fourth quarter, the hard-charging Pistons had moved ahead by 7 points. The Lakers made a final push to tie the contest, but Worthy missed a key free throw down the stretch and Detroit held on to win 108-105. Worse than being in an 0-2 hole, the Lakers would now be without a healthy Magic Johnson, who hurt himself in the game.

Magic tried to start in Game 3, but was forced to the bench after just a few minutes. Refusing to give up, the Lakers hung tough in their floor general's absence, as Cooper took over at the point, and Abdul-Jabbar played with the energy of a rookie. Unfortunately for the home team, Detroit's backcourt was just too much to handle. Dumars scored 17 straight points in the third quarter, and Johnson canned 13 in the fourth. Late in the game, the Lakers had a chance to tie the score with a 3-pointer, but Dumars was right there to block a desperate attempt by rookie David Rivers. Game 4 was tough to watch for the fans at the Forum. They knew it would be Kareem's final appearance in L.A., and they held out little hope that their team would fend off the Pistons at this point. The Lakers surprised them by hanging tough, and with less than two minutes remaining Abdul-Jabbar hit a shot—the last of his fabled career—to make the game close. But Laimbeer answered with a jumper that put the game on ice, and Detroit won 105-97.

Pistons 4
Lakers 0
MVP: Isiah Thomas, Detroit

CHAPTER 5

THE 1990s

1990
Detroit Pistons vs. Portland Trailblazers

The Bad Boys made good on their goal of repeating as Eastern Conference champs in the spring of 1990. The face of the team changed somewhat when Rick Mahorn was lost in the league's expansion draft, but coach Chuck Daly still had plenty of muscle and attitude to work with. He discovered Detroit was stronger with Mark Aguirre and John Salley coming off the bench, so Dennis Rodman and James Edwards were inserted into the starting lineup alongside center Bill Laimbeer. In the backcourt, Isiah Thomas and Joe Dumars offered a unique mix of offense and defense, and Vinnie Johnson continued to live up to his reputation as the Microwave. Throughout the year, the Pistons encountered tough competition in the Central Division from Michael Jordan and the Chicago Bulls. Detroit finished the regular season with a record of 59-23. In the playoffs, after the team breezed past the Indiana Pacers and New York Knicks, the Bulls came knocking again. The Pistons were ready, but it took them seven hard games to keep Michael Jordan and company out of the finals.

In the West, the Portland Trailblazers were an up-and-coming team that found the veteran leadership it needed in forward Buck Williams. He joined a young and energetic frontcourt made up of Jerome Kersey and Kevin Duckworth. Portland's two best players were guards Clyde "The Glide" Drexler and Terry Porter, and coach Rick Adelman encouraged them to freelance all over the court. The top scorers off the bench were forward Cliff Robinson and guard Drazen Petrovic, a deadly jumpshooter from Yugoslavia. The Trailblazers pushed the Los Angeles Lakers all season long, finishing second in the Pacific Division at 59-23. They beat the Dallas Mavericks easily in the first round of the postseason, then watched with relief as the Phoenix Suns upset the Lakers. Portland defeated the San Antonio Spurs in a seven-game series and took care of the Suns in six.

More than anyone else on the Detroit team, Thomas had something to prove entering the series against the Trailblazers. Many fans believed his game had slipped. Thomas waited until the perfect moment to show them they were wrong. With the Pistons down by 10 points in the final period of Game 1 at Detroit's Palace, the point guard produced a furious scoring barrage that turned the contest around. Thomas netted 33 points, including 10 in the crucial fourth quarter, to spark a 105-99 victory. In Game 2, the Pistons broke out on top, but this time Portland fought back. Thanks to clutch shooting from Drexler and Porter, the Trailblazers sent the contest to overtime. When Laimbeer hit a 3-pointer late in the extra period, it appeared the Pistons would escape with a win. But Rodman

Isiah Thomas surveys the defense as he brings the ball up the court. The Detroit point guard was sensational against Portland in the 1990 finals.

fouled Drexler on Portland's last possession, and the 6'7" guard sunk two free throws for a 106-105 victory.

As the series shifted to Portland for the next three contests, the Trailblazers were understandably optimistic. Detroit, however, made them rethink their position with a 121-106 shellacking in Game 3. Dumars, who learned afterwards that his father had died, was the star with 33 points. In Game 4, Thomas scored 22 points in the third quarter to spearhead a big run by Detroit, but the Trailblazers stormed back. With time running out, reserve Danny Young launched a long three-pointer. The ball went in, but officials ruled that it had left Young's hand after the buzzer sounded. Instead of facing tie game and overtime, Detroit walked away a 112-109 winner. Game 5 ended in heartbreak for Blazer fans, as well. As the clock wound down in a 90-90 game, Thomas passed to Johnson who let go from 15 feet. When the line drive hit its mark, Detroit had won another barnburner to claim its second title in a row. Thomas, who silenced his critics by averaging 27.6 points and 8 assists for the series, was named MVP.

Pistons 4
Trailblazers 1
MVP: Isiah Thomas, Detroit

1991
Chicago Bulls vs. Los Angeles Lakers

Entering the 1990-91 campaign, 27-year-old Michael Jordan had already claimed five scoring titles and an MVP in his NBA career. He had yet to capture a championship, however, and that's what he craved most of all. This year, Jordan had every reason to believe his Bulls could go all the way. Chicago was returning the same starting five that had come close to a win for a place in the finals, and the club had finally bought into coach Phil Jackson's defensive-minded style of play. Forward Scottie Pippen was blossoming into a great all-around player, and Horace Grant was the prototype NBA power forward. They worked beautifully with centers Bill Cartwright and Will Perdue. In the backcourt, John Paxson's timely shooting made him the perfect complement to Jordan, who was roundly hailed as the greatest basketball player anyone had ever seen. Chicago's bench, led by guard B.J. Armstrong, was deep and ready whenever called upon. The Bulls ascended to the top of the Central Division with a record of 61-21. When the post-season began, they raised their game another notch, disposing of the New York Knicks, Philadelphia 76ers, and Detroit Pistons with remarkable ease.

Out West, the Los Angeles Lakers, now under the guidance of coach Mike Dunleavy, returned to the finals after a year's hiatus. The heart of the team was still the incomparable Magic Johnson, who got plenty of help from James Worthy. The Lakers also benefited from the addition of two new starters, free-agent signee Sam Perkins and Yugoslavian center Vlade Divac, promoted from his back-up role when Kareem Abdul-Jabbar departed. Though Byron Scott had a down year, Terry Teagle provided a spark off the bench. A.C. Green also made his presence felt in a reserve role. After finishing second in the Pacific Division at 58-24, Los Angeles hit its stride in the playoffs. A

sweep of the Houston Rockets was followed by solid series wins over the Golden State Warriors and Portland Trailblazers.

The league billed the finals as a battle between Jordan and Johnson, despite the fact they were unlikely to spend much time going one-on-one. For his part, Jordan planned to play more like Magic, setting up his teammates whenever possible and only taking shots when they were there for him. In past years, this strategy would have likely ended in disaster. The Bulls, in awe of their young superstar, spent a lot of time standing around wondering what incredible thing he would do next. When Jackson designed an offense that kept them more involved, the team's performance became much more consistent and the pressure on Jordan to pump in 40 points every night ended. In Game 1, at Chicago Stadium, Jordan did indeed share the ball, but the experience of the Lakers won out. With time winding down, they worked the ball to Perkins, who nailed a three-pointer that put Los Angeles up by two. When Jordan missed a game-tying attempt on the other end, L.A. had a nifty 93-91 victory.

Jordan's unselfish play was the key in Game 2. In a 107-86 laugher, the Bulls shot an amazing 73 percent from the floor, including an 8-of-8 performance by Paxson. When the series moved West to the Forum, Johnson and his cohorts expected to seize control. But Jordan shocked them in Game 3 with a last-second jumper to send the contest into overtime. In the extra period, the Bulls scored eight straight points to seal a 104-96 victory. Game 4 featured a defensive clinic by the Bulls, who embarrassed L.A., 97-82. In Game 5, Jordan poured it on, gliding through the Laker defense for easy shots and crisp passes to wide-open teammates. Pippen led all scorers with 32 points and Paxson chipped in 20 as the Bulls cruised to a 108-101 win and their first championship.

> Bulls 4
> Lakers 1
> MVP: Michael Jordan, Chicago

1992
Chicago Bulls vs.
Portland Trailblazers

Michael Jordan now understood what it took to win a championship. That knowledge would prove invaluable as he defended his crown. Under Jordan's tutelage, Scottie Pippen had developed into the league's best forward. His mates on the front line, Horace Grant and Bill Cartwright, contributed strong rebounding and tough defense. John Paxson and B.J. Armstrong shared time at the point, each content to provide hand-in-glove support for Jordan, who won another scoring title and his second straight MVP award. Coach Phil Jackson used his reserves with great intelligence, inserting players like Stacey King and Cliff Levingston when the starters looked stale. For much of the regular season, the Bulls looked like they might break the NBA record for wins, but eventually settled for 67. Their toughest challenge in the playoffs came from the New York Knicks, who pushed them to 7 games in the second round. That series victory was sandwiched between a sweep of the Miami Heat and a six-game victory over the Cleveland Cavaliers.

The Portland Trailblazers, meanwhile, were eager for another shot at a title. The starting five from the club that advanced to the 1990 finals was now older and wiser. In the backcourt, high-flying Clyde Drexler combined with Terry Porter, a point guard with a shooter's mentality. Jerome Kersey, Buck Williams, and Kevin Duckworth formed a frontline that was solid, but not spectacular. Forward Cliff Robinson had matured a great deal and provided instant offense off the bench. Reserve guard Danny Ainge was not shy with the ball in his hands, either. Coach Rick Adelman led his troops to a record of 57-25 and their second consecutive Pacific Division crown. Portland then marched through the playoffs, defeating the Los Angeles Lakers (who lost Magic Johnson after he was diagnosed with the HIV virus), Phoenix Suns, and Utah Jazz in succession.

Despite their tremendous record, the Bulls entered the finals in a bit of turmoil. Teammates had begun to gripe about the preferential treatment shown to Jordan by Jackson. The Chicago superstar was blunt in his assertion that this was neither the time nor the place for such complaints. For his part, Jackson secretly liked the fact his players were a little on edge. He channeled this energy into a great performance in Game 1, a 122-89 blowout of the Blazers that featured a 35-point first half by Jordan. Portland proved its resilience in Game 2, scoring a 115-104 overtime win. Ainge, the ex-Celtic, netted 9 points in the extra period. In Portland for the next three contests, Chicago reassumed control of the series. In Game 3, Jordan's 26 points topped a balanced scoring attack in a 94-84 victory by the Bulls. The resilient Trailblazers fought back with a gutsy effort in Game 4, beating Chicago 93-88.

TEAM SPIRIT
THE 1990s: CHICAGO BULLS

Michael Jordan starred for the Chicago Bulls for several years before the team became a legitimate championship contender. In fact, it was not until the Bulls became a team that Jordan started winning NBA titles. Under coaches Kevin Loughery, Stan Albeck, and Doug Collins, the superstar put on a show every night, but his teammates were often among the spectators. You could beat the Bulls by letting Jordan score 40 and then shutting down the rest of the Chicago players.

The pieces started coming together when talented role players such as Charles Oakley, Horace Grant, John Paxson, and Bill Cartwright were added to the roster in the late 1980s. Forward Scottie Pippen, whom the Bulls stole from the Seattle Supersonics, blossomed into a frontline defensive star and developed quickly as a second scorer.

Coach Phil Jackson, a reserve on the great Knicks teams of the 1970s, was hired to stir this mixture of talent and produce a winner. He borrowed from Zen philosophy and Red Holzman's handbook to create a team concept that allowed Jordan to do what he did best, while keeping everyone else involved in ways Jackson knew they would be successful. The Bulls did not have a star center, nor did they have a point guard—normally a recipe for disaster. But Jackson's clever "Triangle" offense worked around this deficiency by letting Jordan and Pippen play floor general. On defense, all of the Bulls played smart and played hard.

In Jackson's second season at the helm, the Bulls captured the NBA championship. Chicago won it all the next two years, then Jordan took a break from basketball. Although the Bulls did not reach the finals during his absence, they did win more than 60 percent of their games. When Jordan rejoined the club, a new cast of support players was in place. Jordan and Pippen—backed up by Dennis Rodman, Steve Kerr, Luc Longley, Ron Harper, and Toni Kukoc—won three more championships.

Jordan made Game 5 his personal showcase. Going to the hoop time and again, he piled up 46 points en route to a 119-106 win. Back at Chicago Stadium for Game 6, the Bulls came out flat as a pancake. With his team down by 17 points in the third quarter, a frustrated Jackson pulled all of his starters except for Pippen and kept his fingers crossed. The unorthodox strategy worked, and the reserves battled back. With eight minutes left and the contest up for grabs, he reinserted Jordan, who put the finishing touches on a 97-93 victory.

Bulls 4
Trailblazers 2
MVP: Michael Jordan, Chicago

1993
Chicago Bulls vs. Phoenix Suns

Michael Jordan and the Bulls were hoping to accomplish what no team since the Celtics of the 1960s had done: win three straight NBA championships. This challenge fueled Jordan and Scottie Pippen, who had little time to rest after the 1992 finals. Both agreed to join USA Basketball's Olympic "Dream Team," which won a gold medal in the Barcelona Summer Games. Not surprisingly, these two stars suffered through some sluggish stretches during the 1992-93 campaign, and the Bulls' record dropped to 57-25. But once the post-season rolled around, Jordan, Pippen, and the rest of the Chicago club were ready for action. The team had undergone relatively little change, save for the addition of B.J. Armstrong to the starting lineup and minutes at play for big man Scott Williams. The Atlanta Hawks and Cleveland Cavaliers provided little competition for the Bulls in the first two rounds, while the Knicks extended Chicago to six games before bowing out.

The Phoenix Suns had a Dream Team star of their own. Charles Barkley, acquired from the Philadelphia 76ers, proved to be the missing ingredient for a team that had plenty of talent but no dominant star. Kevin Johnson, Dan Majerle, and backup Danny Ainge gave the Suns an excellent backcourt, while Cedric Ceballos, Mark West, Richard Dumas, and Tom Chambers joined Barkley on the front line. Coach Paul Westphal spread the minutes around and kept everyone happy on the way to an NBA-best 62-win season. Phoenix edged the Los Angeles Lakers, San Antonio Spurs, and Seattle Su-

Charles Barkley is a picture of concentration on the front of his 1992 Topps Stadium trading card. Always popular with collectors, Barkley generated even more interest after leading the Suns to the NBA finals.

personics, finding a way to deal with match-up problems in each series.

The match-up Phoenix feared against the Bulls was Jordan. Their only hope was that a growing controversy surrounding his love of high-stakes gambling would distract him in the finals. This was not the case in Game 1, which Chicago won 100-92 at Phoenix's America West Arena. Jordan scored 31 points, while his teammates frustrated Barkley. The big forward was more of a factor in Game 2, but the Bulls countered by clamping down on guards Johnson and Majerle. Jordan dropped 42 on the Suns in an exciting 111-108 victory. Game 3 was the best of the series, as Phoenix regrouped and pushed the Bulls into triple-overtime on their own home court. Johnson was the key for the Suns with 25 points and nine assists. The tough little playmaker was on the floor for a record 62 minutes to lead his team to a 129-121 win.

Jordan responded in Game 4 with 55 points to lead a 111-105 victory. This gave Chicago fans hope that their Bulls would win a third title before the series headed back West. But Phoenix spoiled the fun in Game 5 as Barkley and Johnson played brilliantly in a 108-98 triumph. With the remaining contests scheduled at home, the Suns held out a slim hope that they might win in seven games. They made a spirited attempt at extending the series in Game 6, matching the Bulls shot for shot until they

had a four-point lead with 90 seconds left. Jordan cut the deficit in half with a short jumper, then the Bulls got the ball back with time winding down. They whipped it around until John Paxson snuck back behind the three-point line all alone to receive a pass. The veteran calmly nailed the long shot to put the Bulls up by one. Johnson made a final attempt to win it for Phoenix, but Grant was there to swat his shot away and the Bulls were 99-98 winners.

> Bulls 4
> Suns 2
> MVP: Michael Jordan, Chicago

1994
New York Knicks vs. Houston Rockets

Just when they were looking unbeatable, the Chicago Bulls were stunned to discover that they would be playing the 1993-94 season without Michael Jordan. Upset by the gambling allegations leveled at him the previous spring, devastated by the murder of his father during the summer, and perhaps just tired of the grind of pro basketball, the superstar announced he was retiring from the Bulls to pursue a baseball career. Suddenly, the NBA championship was up for grabs.

In the West, the Houston Rockets had assembled a good team under coach Rudy Tomjanovich. Hakeem Olajuwon had blossomed into an agile, multitalented pivot man. Forwards Otis Thorpe, Robert Horry, and Mario Elie gave opponents all kinds of trouble, while fleet-footed Kenny Smith, trash-talking Vernon Maxwell, and clutch-shooting Sam Cassell gave the Rockets an

Phil Jackson and Michael Jordan congratulate each other on the Bulls' 1993 NBA championship. They would win three more together after Jordan's brief retirement from the game.

explosive backcourt. Houston finished atop the Midwest Division with a 58-24 record. In the post-season, the Rockets defeated the Portland Trailblazers, Phoenix Suns, and Utah Jazz to advance to the finals.

The New York Knicks were the team expected to fill the void if the Bulls faltered, and they lived up to those expectations. They won the Atlantic Division behind a great year from center Patrick Ewing, who led a cast of tough guys that included forwards Charles Oakley, Anthony Mason, and guards Derek Harper and John Starks. Coach Pat Riley, who bemoaned the ruination of basketball when his Lakers were trampled by Detroit, now coached a team that was every bit as hard-nosed as the old Pistons. What the Knicks lacked in depth they gained in the clutch play of Ewing, who did it all, every night, at both ends of the floor. New York beat the Nets in the opening round of the playoffs, then overcame the Bulls in seven games with some help from the referees. Reggie Miller and the Indiana Pacers put up a great fight in a series that went the distance, but the Knicks survived to earn a date with the Rockets.

Aficionados of "big" basketball relished the showdown between Olajuwon and Ewing. They were the last great centers from the 1980s, and their teams revolved around them the way George Mikan's Lakers had around him four decades earlier. Olajuwon won the war in Game 1 at the Houston Summit, scoring 28 points on the way to an 85-78 victory. The next night, Starks came to life with 19 points, and Harper nailed a pair of three-pointers down the stretch as New York held on, 91-83. When the series moved to Madison Square Garden for the next three contests, Houston got a spark from Cassell, who scored seven points in the final 33 sec-

Hakeem Olajuwon and Patrick Ewing clash in the low post. The 1994 finals came down to a battle of the big men.

onds to win Game 3 for the Rockets, 93-89. The Knicks were in deep trouble in Game 4, trailing in the third quarter with the Rockets poised to make a run. But Starks and Harper got hot from long range, and New York knotted the series at 2-2 with a 91-82 win.

Game 5 belonged to Ewing, who spearheaded the offense with 25 points and played tough defense against Olajuwon in a 91-84 victory. The series went back West with the Knicks needing just one win for the championship. Game 6 went down to the wire, with Houston up 84-82 and time running out. Starks lined up a three-pointer to win the champions for New York, but Olajuwon came flying out of the paint to deflect his shot and preserve the victory. The Knicks kept going to Starks in Game 7, which proved a grave mistake. The hot-handed guard went cold, and by the time Ewing took charge of the offense it was too late. Olajuwon and Maxwell were terrific, and the Rockets hung on to win 90-84 and collect the first championship in franchise history.

> **Rockets 4**
> **Knicks 3**
> **MVP: Hakeem Olajuwon, Houston**

1995
Orlando Magic vs. Houston Rockets

Midway through the 1994-95 season, the Houston Rockets looked like they had no chance to repeat as NBA champions. The team was in disarray, and a blockbuster trade with Portland seemed only to make matters worse. Power forward Otis Thorpe was shipped to the Trailblazers with a draft choice for Clyde Drexler, who at 32 had lost some of his glide. Shooting guards Vernon Maxwell and Mario Elie were unhappy, knowing that they would lose time to Drexler, and fans wondered who would line up next to Hakeem Olajuwon under the boards with Thorpe gone. Coach Rudy Tomjanovich solved these problems by switching three guards, and spotting Carl Herrera and Pete Chilcutt in the power forward slot. Kenny Smith and Sam Cassell handled the point, and Olajuwon had a great year playing with Drexler, his old college teammate. The Rockets came together by season's end and upended the Utah Jazz in the first round of the playoffs. After that, the Suns and Spurs fell as the Rockets reached the finals looking for an unlikely repeat.

Their opponent, the Orlando Magic, starred two of the NBA's most dynamic young players. Penny Hardaway, a 6'7" guard in just his second pro season, ran the team like a veteran from the perimeter, from where he could shoot, pass, or penetrate depending on what defense gave him. They gave him a lot, because their main concern was the man in the middle, Shaquille O'Neal. "Shaq" moved like a man six inches shorter and 60 pounds lighter than his 7'2", 300-pound frame. This made him virtually unstoppable when he got the ball near the basket. O'Neal was still learning the ropes as an NBA center, but he was already the top point-producer in the game. Coach Brian Hill surrounded these two with capable players, including ex-Bull Horace Grant, sharpshooting Nick Anderson and Dennis Scott, and bench players Donald Royal and Brian Shaw. The Magic had little trouble defeating the Celtics in the first round of the playoffs, but everyone assumed Chicago—who had Michael Jordan again after he came out of retirement—would beat Orlando in the playoffs. Shaq and company were too much for the rusty Bulls, however, who fell in six games. The Magic got more of a fight from the Pacers, who played them incredibly close until they finally blew them out in the seventh game of the Eastern Conference finals.

As the second half of Game 1 got under way, it looked like there would be a changing of the guard in the NBA. The Magic, playing at home, were destroying the Rockets. Before the third quarter ended, Orlando had a 20-point lead. Finally, Smith heated up for the Rockets and began nailing shot after shot. This spread the floor for Olajuwon, who taught Shaq a thing or two in the paint. Houston made a great comeback and pushed the game into overtime. With the score tied and time running out, Drexler

"Penny" and "Shaq" share an NBA Hoops trading card from their days with the Magic. They were among the most sought after players in the hobby.

1996
Chicago Bulls vs. Seattle Supersonics

The fun was over in 1995-96. Michael Jordan regained his form and the Bulls—who had learned to win without him—were practically unbeatable. Phil Jackson had reassembled the team to revolve equally around Jordan and Scottie Pippen, who was now one of the top players in the league. Among the new faces were rebounding fiend Dennis Rodman, a 6-11 swingman from Croatia named Toni Kukoc, Australian center Luc Longley and point guards Steve Kerr and Ron Harper. The Bulls beat you on offense, defense, under the backboards, and beyond the arc. No one could solve this team. Jordan reclaimed the scoring title and MVP, and Chicago finished with a new NBA record for victories with 72. In the playoffs, the Bulls stomped the Miami Heat, New York Knicks, and Orlando Magic for a shot at another championship.

The Seattle Supersonics, who combined experience, athleticism, and attitude, proved the best in the West in 1995-96. Coach George Karl had top-notch starters in point guard Gary Payton and power forward Shawn Kemp, and a roster loaded with above-average role players. Detlef Schrempf, Sam Perkins, and Hersey Hawkins could score 20 a night if needed, while Ervin Johnson, Vincent Askew, and Nate McMillan were good defenders. The Sonics finished in first place in the Pacific Division with a record of 64-18. In the post-season, they took care of the Sacramento Kings and Houston Rockets with ease, then nosed past the Utah Jazz in seven games.

To subdue Jordan, Karl assigned Schrempf to guard him one-on-one and instructed Hawkins to help out whenever possible. The

missed a shot but Olajuwon tipped it in for a 120-118 victory. Olajuwon won the battle of the big men again in Game 2, burning O'Neal for 34 points. Cassell chipped in 31 for a 117-106 victory that sent the series to Houston. Horry hit a clutch three-pointer to seal a 106-103 victory in Game 3, and Elie scored 22 in Game 4 to lead the Rockets to a 113-101 win and a stunning sweep.

> Rockets 4
> Magic 0
> MVP: Hakeem Olajuwon, Houston

strategy worked for a while in Game 1, but all the attention the Sonics paid to Jordan caught up with them in the fourth quarter, as the other Bulls began to hit their open shots. With Kukoc scoring 10 points in a row to start the period, Chicago cruised to a 107-90 victory before a noisy home crowd at the United Center. Seattle managed to contain Jordan in Game 2, but again they were victimized by another Bulls. This time it was Rodman, who yanked down an offensive rebound at the end of the game, then made an important free throw to seal Chicago's 92-88 win.

When the series shifted to Seattle's Key Arena, the Sonics slacked off Jordan, who erupted for 36 points in a demoralizing 108-86 win. Down 3 games to 0, Seattle fought back for a pair of wins, but the Bulls got serious back in Chicago and rallied behind Jordan in Game 6 to suffocate the Sonic of-

fense. The contest, played on Father's Day, held special meaning for number 23, who had dedicated the series to the memory of his dad. After the buzzer sounded on Chicago's 87-75 win, Jordan hugged the trophy and began to cry.

> Bulls 4
> Sonics 2
> MVP: Michael Jordan, Chicago

1997
Chicago Bulls vs. Utah Jazz

Despite injuries to Dennis Rodman, Toni Kukoc, and Luc Longley, the Chicago Bulls were every bit as good as they had been during their record-smashing 1995-96 season. Michael Jordan and Scottie Pippen were sensational, and role players Steve Kerr, Ron Harper, Jason Caffey, and Randy Brown got the job done for coach Phil Jackson all year long. The Bulls finished with 69 victories, then obliterated the Washington Bullets, Atlanta Hawks, and Miami Heat for a return trip to the finals.

Their opponents would be a team that had been knocking on the door since the 1980s, but had never made it to the NBA's big dance. The Utah Jazz, led by John Stockton and Karl "The Mailman" Malone, finally made the finals after wining 64 games and defeating the Clippers, Lakers, and Rockets in the playoffs. Stockton, a playmaking guard who seemed to sense things on the court a beat before everyone else, ran an offense built around Malone, the most complete power forward in basket-

Gary Payton of the Sonics attempts to contain Michael Jordan. The Bulls' superstar was at his best in the series as Chicago won in six games.

THE 1990s • 83

ball history. The supporting class included tough and talented Jeff Hornacek, Howard Eisley, and Shandon Anderson at guard, forwards Byron Russell and Antoine Carr, and center Greg Ostertag. Jerry Sloan molded this group into a tenacious, winning team.

Game 1, in Chicago, came down to Malone and Jordan. In the closing moments, both were presented with a chance to win the game. Malone missed two vital free throws, while Jordan sank a 19-footer when it was his turn to play hero, and the Bulls won 84-82. Jordan was all over the place in Game 2, with 36 points, 13 rebounds, and nine assists in a 97-85 win. Utah was too good to panic, even down 0-2. The Jazz took Game 3 at the Delta Center by a score of 104-93 and then emerged in a 78-73 defensive struggle in Game 4. The key play in the second contest was a gorgeous length-of-the-court pass from Stockton to Malone that the Mailman turned into an easy bucket.

Game 5 saw Jordan add to his legend as basketball's greatest ever. Weakened by a stomach ailment, he seemed helpless to rally his troops against the resurgent Jazz. Utah built a 16-point lead and seemed poised to take a 3 games to 2 series lead. As the game neared its conclusion, Jordan reached down and found a little extra. By the final minute of the game the Bulls had regained the lead, and their star slammed the lid on the shell-shocked Jazz with a final three-pointer in a 90-88 victory. Game 6 found the two clubs back in the Windy City, where Jordan and Malone pushed their teammates into the final minutes with the score seesawing back and forth. With the score tied 86-86, the Bulls got the ball and Sloan ordered his players to double-team Jordan. As soon as the second defender arrived, Jordan spotted Kerr all alone on the perimeter. He delivered a perfect pass, Kerr hit the shot, and the Bulls went on to win, 90-86.

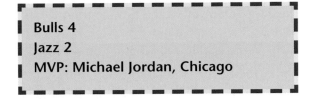

Bulls 4
Jazz 2
MVP: Michael Jordan, Chicago

1998
Chicago Bulls vs. Utah Jazz

With retirement on his mind, Michael Jordan was determined to make his last NBA season a memorable one. He led the league in scoring and played all 82 games for the Bulls, who won 62 times for Phil Jackson. The same cast of characters was on hand for a run at Chicago's sixth title, with the addition of swingman Scott Burrell, who like Jordan had also tried his hand a professional baseball. Scottie Pippen, Toni Kukoc, Luc Longley, and Dennis Rodman logged the majority of the minutes in the frontcourt, while Ron Harper, Steve Kerr, and Randy Brown played beside Jordan in the backcourt. The Bulls beat the New Jersey Nets and Charlotte Hornets in the first two rounds of the playoffs, before the Indiana Pacers tested them in a seven-game series.

The Utah Jazz returned to the finals hoping to even the score with Chicago. Jerry Sloan's men had replayed the previous year's series in their minds so many times, and had convinced themselves that only a couple of key plays had kept them from winning. John Stockton and Karl Malone won 62 games with virtually the same team. Jeff Hornacek, Byron Russell, and Adam Keefe filled out the starting five, with Greg Ostertag now coming off the bench. Utah's reserves included Shandon Anderson, Howard Eisley, Greg Foster, and Antoine Carr. After a brutal series with the Rockets, the Jazz steamrolled the San Antonio Spurs and the fast-improving Los Angeles Lakers for a return date with Jordan and the Bulls.

Armed with the homecourt advantage, the Jazz felt confident entering the finals. Game 1 emboldened them further when they won 88-85 in overtime, despite a sub-par performance from Malone. The Mailman did not deliver in Game 2 either, and this time it cost the Jazz a victory, as Jordan and company evened the series by a score of 93-88. The Bulls turned up the defensive pressure when they returned to Chicago's United Center. They held Utah to an embarrassing 54 points in a 96-54 blowout, and took the swagger out of the Jazz, who had been counting on winning two games on the road. The Bulls put an end to that possibility when Pippen drained five three-pointers on the way to an 86-82 win that put the Jazz in a 1-3 hole.

The Jazz looked to Malone in Game 5, and he finally came through. Snapping out of the doldrums, he scorched the Bulls with 39 points, leading Utah to an 83-81 victory and setting up Game 6 in the Delta Center. Technically, the Jazz had regained the homecourt advantage, but no one really believed that—least of all Jordan, who knew he had to shoulder more of the load with Pippen's back bothering him. In a tightly contested Game 6, Jordan hit several big shots but the Bulls still trailed heading into the fourth quarter. The Jazz played tough, and held a slim lead with time running out. Jordan made a driving layup to cut the deficit to 86-85, then stole the ball from Malone to give the Bulls one last shot. As the last seconds ticked away, Jordan went one-on-one with Russell. As they neared the foul line, Jordan

faked a move to the basket, then rose straight into the air as Russell reeled backward. The ball touched nothing but net, and for the second time, the Bulls had won three championships in a row. If Michael Jordan's plan was to go out with a flourish, he could not have written himself a better part.

Bulls 4
Jazz 2
MVP: Michael Jordan, Chicago

1999
New York Knicks vs. San Antonio Spurs

A bitter labor dispute cut deeply into the 1998-99 NBA season, reducing the schedule to a mere 50 games. This created a wild sprint to the finish, as teams hastily trained, players worked themselves into shape during the season, and many free agent signees joined their teams after the games had begun. The shortened schedule favored teams with experienced veterans, as they would not be as tired at playoff time. This theory held true for the San Antonio Spurs, a club with older stars like David Robinson, Sean Elliott, Avery Johnson, and Mario Elie. The player who put the Spurs over the top, however, was young Tim Duncan. The agile power forward had earned first-team All-NBA honors his first two years in the league, and he seemed to improve each week. Coach Gregg Popovich had a good bench, playoff-tested Steve Kerr and Jerome Kersey, as well as Jaren Jackson. The Spurs finished 37-13, tying them with the Utah Jazz for the top spot in the Midwest Division. In the playoffs, the Spurs beat Kevin Garnett and the Minnesota Timberwolves, then Robinson and Duncan doubled up on Shaquille O'Neal to defeat the Los Angeles Lakers. Portland posed little problem after that, and San Antonio was in the finals.

The New York Knicks were far less glamorous. Comprised of a hodgepodge of troubled stars and over-the-hill veterans, this group staggered through a 27-23 regular season before coming together in the playoffs. Jeff Van Gundy's two best players were Latrell Sprewell and Allan Houston; who happened to play the same position, shooting guard. This created more problems for opponents than for the Knicks, so they just rolled with it. The front line consisted of ancient Patrick Ewing, oft-injured Marcus Camby and Larry Johnson, and Kurt Thomas, a great college scorer who had yet to find his niche in the NBA. Charlie Ward, a former Heisman Trophy-winning quarterback, ran the point along with streaky Chris Childs, who had a knack for hitting big shots. The Knicks survived a violent opening-round series with the hated Miami Heat, then beat the Hawks. Against the heavily favored Indiana Pacers, New York survived an intense, six-game series to find themselves playing for the NBA championship.

With two older, defensive-minded teams in the finals, the series figured to be a low-scoring, grind-it-out affair. Game 1 followed this script, as the Knicks managed just 10 points in the second quarter. Duncan proved the difference-maker, as he scored 33 points and grabbed 16 rebounds in an 89-77 Spurs win. New York's offensive woes continued in Game 2, as the team made just 27 of its 82 shots during the game. Duncan was the star once again, as San Antonio bashed its way to an ugly 80-67 victory.

When the series moved to New York's Madison Square Garden, the Knicks finally found their rhythm. In Game 3, Houston exploded for 13 points in the first quarter on his way to a game-high 34, and led New York to an 89-81 win. The Spurs almost overwhelmed the Knicks in Game 4, as Duncan and Robinson had their way under the boards and Elie, Johnson, and Elliott lit it up from outside. New York mounted a furious comeback, but San Antonio held on, 96-89. The Knicks' only chance in Game 5 was to slow the pace to a crawl. Duncan starred again, but Sprewell and Houston kept their team close. They could not hit a shot down the stretch, however, and the Spurs won the championship on a jumper by Johnson, 78-77.

Spurs 4
Knicks 1
MVP: Tim Duncan, San Antonio

Tim Duncan of the Spurs rises over Knick defender Marcus Camby. San Antonio beat New York in five games.

CHAPTER 6

2000 AND BEYOND

2000
Indiana Pacers vs.
Los Angeles Lakers

Not since Magic Johnson was running the team in the 1980s had the Los Angeles Lakers gotten close to an NBA. The club had rebuilt since then, and had an excellent core of players, but still they could not win. The last piece of the puzzle was Phil Jackson. He left coaching when Michael Jordan retired, but was lured back by the prospect of molding the twin talents of Shaquille O'Neal and Kobe Bryant into championship form. He realized in training camp that his two stars had to work together for the team to reach the next level, and explained to Bryant that a championship offense went through its center. The 21-year-old agreed to defer to Shaq, and suddenly all was well in Laker land. In Los Angeles, Jackson was working with even better support than he had in Chicago. Glen Rice, Derek Fisher, Brian Shaw, and ex-Bull Ron Harper joined Bryant in the backcourt, while the forwards included Rick Fox, Robert Horry, and A.C Green. The team concentrated more on defense and rebounding, and Kobe began doing the little things needed to earn his teammates' trust. The result was the league's best record at

Shaquille O'Neal rejects a shot by Indiana's Jalen Rose. "Shaq" made the difference in what would be the first of three consecutive Laker championships.

67-15. The Sacramento Kings gave the Lakers a scare in the first round of the playoffs, and after the Suns went quietly, the Portland Trailblazers also played L.A. tough. As far as Jackson was concerned, his team was just rounding into form.

The Indiana Pacers also had a coach who knew something about winning titles. Larry Bird returned to his native Indiana to coach a team that always seemed to come up one win short in the post-season. This time, he got them to the finals. Bird's top offensive weapons were Jalen Rose and Reggie Miller, both of whom could score from anywhere on the court. Point guard Mark Jackson could distribute the ball, or back into the basket and post-up an unsuspecting defender. Travis Best provided instant offense off the bench, while forwards Dale Davis, Sam Perkins, and Austin Croshere flanked willowy Rick Smits at center. The Pacers won 56 games, then out-dueled the Bucks, 76ers, and Knicks to rate a date with the heavily favored Lakers.

Indiana's primary objective in the finals was to throw O'Neal off his game. They hoped to accomplish this by giving him a different defensive look almost every time down the floor. If he had to hesitate in order to recognize what he was up against, Bird reasoned, it might disrupt his rhythm. Shaq proved quicker than the Pacers anticipated, however, making his move before they could double-team him. In Game 1, he scorched Indiana for 43 points in a 104-87 victory. Bryant hurt his ankle in Game 2, and the Pacers put even more pressure on O'Neal. He responded by whipping the ball to his open teammates, enabling Rice and Harper to score 21 apiece in a 111-104 win. Miller stepped into the spotlight in Game 3 at Indiana's Conseco Fieldhouse, scoring 33 in a 100-91 Pacer win.

Game 4 was a classic. The key was the return of Bryant, who made several clutch baskets down the stretch to send the game into overtime. Kobe soared even higher in the extra period, and the Lakers won a 120-118 thriller. With their backs against the wall, the Pacers pulled off an astonishing 120-87 triumph in Game 5 to send the series back to L.A. There the Pacers continued their improved play, fashioning a 56-53 halftime advantage. Rose and Jackson kept the pressure on with great third quarters, but the Lakers kept chipping away. They took the lead with nine minutes left, and it was a dogfight the rest of the way. A loose-ball foul by Croshere in the waning moments gave Los Angeles some breathing room, and Bryant hit some clutch free throws to put the game away. When the buzzer sounded on the 116-111 Laker win, Bryant leaped into Shaq's arms.

Lakers 4
Pacers 2
MVP: Shaquille O'Neal, Los Angeles

2001
Philadelphia 76ers vs. Los Angeles Lakers

The only thing that could keep Shaquille O'Neal and Kobe Bryant from winning another championship was Shaquille O'Neal and Kobe Bryant. The two renewed their love-hate relationship when the 2000-01 season began, and it took Phil Jackson most of the year to smooth out their feelings. In the interim, the supporting cast of Rick Fox, Brian Shaw, Robert Horry, and Derek Fisher got a year better at doing what they had done a year before. An important newcomer to the club was Horace Grant, an old Jackson favorite acquired in a deal for Glen Rice. Los Angeles had its ups and downs, finishing atop the Pacific Division with 56 wins. But come playoff time, the Lakers shifted into another gear. The Portland Trailblazers, Sacramento Kings, and San Antonio Spurs never knew what hit them, as Shaq, Kobe, and the gang reached the finals without dropping a single game.

The team waiting for them was the Philadelphia 76ers, coached by Larry Brown and led by meteoric Allen Iverson. The 6'0" guard could score every time he touched the ball, and sometimes it seemed as if that was his plan. He had grown up a lot since coming into the league, involving his teammates more and creating a bit less controversy off the court. But the young man they called "The Answer" was still a force of nature. By surrounding Iverson with the likes of Tyrone Hill, Aaron McKie, Eric Snow, and Raja Bell, coach Brown successfully harnessed this force. The addition of shot-blocking center Dikembe Mutombo gave the 76ers just enough to rise to the top of the Atlantic Division. After trouncing the the Pacers in the first round, Philly went to the brink against the Toronto Raptors and Milwaukee Bucks, but survived a pair of Game 7's to reach the finals.

With the whole world betting on a Laker win, the 76ers shocked the crowd in L.A. by matching their team basket-for-basket. Iverson poured in 41 points in regulation to send the game into overtime, then added 7 more in the extra period to take a 1-0 lead in the series with a 107-101 victory. The Lakers woke up in Game 2 and played serious, workmanlike basketball to get back on track. Bryant netted 31 and O'Neal scored 28 in a 98-89 win.

As the series moved to Philadelphia's First Union Center, the 76ers felt optimistic about their chances. The Lakers quickly curbed their enthusiasm, taking Game 3 by a score of 96-91. Once again, Shaq and Kobe were more than Philly could handle. Their hopes of knotting the series ended early the next evening, as L.A. got off to a quick start and led by 17 at the half. The 76ers could not narrow the gap, and fell 100-86. The Lakers closed out the series in Game 5, outplaying Philadelphia in the second and third quarters and holding on to win, 108-96. Though O'Neal won the MVP again, Bryant could just have easily taken top honors. All Jackson cared about was that they were working together. He was already thinking about his third "three-peat."

> Lakers 4
> 76ers 1
> MVP: Shaquille O'Neal, Los Angeles

2002
New Jersey Nets vs. Los Angeles Lakers

Phil Jackson had several months to think about his strategy for the 2001-2002 season. He knew he had a potential 70-win team on his hands, but also sensed that going for the NBA record would burn his guys out. His key veterans—Rick Fox, Robert Horry, and Brian Shaw—knew how to "flick the switch" in the post-season, so what was the point of driving them hard for 82 games? Derek Fisher began the year with an injured foot and Shaquille O'Neal had a sore toe—more reason not to push the Lakers too hard. So Jackson told his guys they were to play hard in the games, but take it easy in practice and

TWO-MAN GAME
KOBE BRYANT AND SHAQUILLE O'NEAL

You don't have to like your fellow superstar to win championships with him. Kobe Bryant, the precocious young guard, and Shaquille O'Neal, the force of nature masquerading as a center, proved this in their championships with the Los Angeles Lakers. Their awesome talent and super-sized egos collided on the court at times, and the fact that the NBA plays with one basketball also made for some problems.

O'Neal, a mammoth center with quickness and attitude, was not able to bring a championship to the Lakers after they signed him as a free agent in the summer of 1996. Bryant, whom Los Angeles acquired one week earlier, was a raw rookie right out of high school who had a lot of growing to do. As Kobe improved, Shaq felt he was no longer the focus of the offense, and a feud erupted between the two.

Coach Phil Jackson, realizing he had two of history's great talents on his roster, finally convinced his pair of stars that if they worked together, they were practically guaranteed a championship. When teams collapsed around O'Neal, Bryant took control. And when opponents went after Bryant, O'Neal destroyed them. Although they did not always see eye-to-eye off the court, Shaq and Kobe found a balance on the court, and the Lakers won it all in 2000, 2001, and 2002.

also off the court. The Lakers glided to a 58-24 record and were happy and healthy when the post-season began. O'Neal and Kobe Bryant were scoring 50 to 60 points a night, and they were just getting revved up.

The surprise club of the NBA awaited the Lakers. The New Jersey Nets had always had talent, but every year injuries seemed to send them into a tailspin. Finally, the whole club was healthy. Kenyon Martin was one of the league's most ferocious defenders, Keith Van Horn was playing with confidence again, and Kerry Kittles was recovered from a devastating knee injury. Coach Byron Scott had an interesting collection of bench players, including veteran Lucious Harris, and hard-working rookies Richard Jefferson and Jason Collins. The Nets also had a solid, stay-at-home center in lumbering Todd MacCulloch. The player who pulled this group together was Jason Kidd, the much-maligned point guard whose enthusiasm had waned after years of playing for lackluster Western Conference clubs. At the beginning of the season, Kidd saw a team that could rebound, run, and play a little D. He eventually convinced his teammates that they could be the best team in the East, and by the spring they were believing him. The Nets picked their way through the playoffs, using

Phil Jackson shares his opinion with a referee as Shaquille O'Neal looks on. Jackson coached the Bulls and Lakers to a total of nine championships between 1991 and 2002.

their opponents' lack of respect as another weapon in their growing arsenal. They beat the Pacers, Hornets, and Celtics in three emotional series to find themselves four wins away from the pinnacle of their sport.

Of course, the Lakers had something to say about that. Having been ambushed a year earlier by Allen Iverson and the 76ers, they had no intention of allowing Kidd to do the same. In Game 1, Shaq put on a clinic, outscoring MacCulloch 40-2. The Lakers built a 23-point lead and fended off a great second-half rally to win 99-94. In Game 2, the Lakers concentrated on snuffing out New Jersey's fast break. They succeeded by having the 6'6" Shaw guard Kidd in the first half, and he went into intermission with no points and only three assists. Reduced to shooting jumpers, the Nets disintegrated and fell 106-83.

After two dispiriting losses out West, the Nets finally played like they were enjoying themselves in front of an extra-loud home crowd in Game 3. Realizing there was no way to handle O'Neal, they concentrated their efforts on Bryant, and enjoyed a fair amount of success. The Nets hit their shots, ran their break, and actually led 86-80 in the fourth quarter. But Bryant caught fire and, as he had in Game 1, squelched New Jersey's hopes with several key buckets. The Lakers escaped with a 106-103 victory. The Nets did not go quietly in Game 4, challenging Shaq and Kobe every time down the floor. But in the end, Los Angeles triumphed, 113-107 for the team's third straight title.

> Lakers 4
> Nets 0
> MVP: Shaquille O'Neal, Los Angeles

2003
New Jersey Nets vs. San Antonio Spurs

The 2002-03 NBA season promised little in the way of surprises when the year began. In the east, the New Jersey Nets had the only club with the kind of balance needed to make a run to the finals. In the west, the Lakers were the favorites, with the improving Sacramento Kings and Dallas Mavericks waiting for the three-time champs to slip up. Almost unnoticed were the Spurs, who at first glance appeared to have too many question marks to contend.

As the season went on, however, the pieces began falling into place. Twenty-year-old Tony Parker took over at point guard, Tim Duncan turned in a second-straight MVP season, and soon-to-retire David "The Admiral" Robinson played with renewed passion. The supporting cast, including Malik Rose, Manu Ginobili, Bruce Bowen, Stephen Jackson, and Speedy Claxton, eased into their roles, and by playoff time San Antonio was playing great basketball. Injuries and indifference hurt the Kings, Mavs, and Lakers, enabling the Spurs to reach the finals.

The Nets did indeed make a return trip to the finals, with Jason Kidd running the show and Kenyon Martin blossoming into a ferocious post-season performer. Forward Richard Jefferson also had a bigger role in the offense, thanks to the departure of Keith Van Horn, who was traded for center Dikembe Mutombo.

The one thing the Nets did not have was an answer for the multitalented Duncan. This became evident in Game One, a defensive war in which Spurs' big man seemed like the only player capable of scoring. The Spurs won that one 84-79, but dropped the next game 87-85 when Kidd turned it up a notch and Duncan missed several clutch free throws. Game Three, in New Jersey, featured horrible shooting (and the lowest-scoring half in finals history), but the Spurs prevailed behind another strong effort from Duncan. Game Four, another low-scoring affair, went to the Nets, 77-76.

With the series knotted 2-2, the Spurs seized control on a magnificent individual performance by Duncan. He scored 29 points in a 93-83 triumph that sent his team back to San Antonio with two chances to close out the Nets. New Jersey led in the fourth quarter of Game Six, but a stunning 19-0 run by the Spurs nailed down the championship. The series established Duncan as the game's best all around player, and gave "The Admiral"—who hauled down 17 rebounds in his last NBA game—a very special bon voyage.

Spurs: 4
Nets: 2
Best Player: Tim Duncan, San Antonio

For Further Information

Lazenby, Roland. *The NBA Finals.* Indianapolis, Indiana: Masters Press,1996.

Pluto, Terry. *Tall Tales.* New York: Simon & Schuster, 1992.

Sachare, Alex. *100 Greatest Basketball Players of All Time.* New York: Pocket Books, 1997.

Salzberg, Charles. *From Set Shot to Slam Dunk.* New York: Dell Publishing, 1987.

Stewart, Mark. *Basketball: A History of Hoops.* Danbury, Connecticut: Franklin Watts, 1998.

Wolff, Alexander. *100 Years of Hoops.* New York: Crescent Books, 1995.

Index

Page numbers in italics indicate illustrations.

About the Author

Mark Stewart ranks among the busiest sportswriters today. He has produced hundreds of profiles on athletes past and present and has authored more than 80 books, including all titles in **The Watts History of Sports.** A graduate of Duke University, Stewart is currently president of Team Stewart, Inc., a sports information and resource company in New Jersey.